Held Together

Carol Mavis Kent

Held Together

The Bonds of the Clark Family

EDITED BY
KAREN MARIE

Healing House
PUBLISHING

First Published in Australia in 2026
by Healing House Publishing
www.healinghousepublishing.com

The National Library of Australia Cataloguing-in-Publication entry:

Title: Held Together
Author: Carol Mavis Kent
Edited by: Karen Marie
Paperback ISBN: 978-1-7641185-9-0

Editor: Vanessa Barrington
Cover and Internal Design: Heidi Glasson

Healing House Publishing is committed to publishing works of quality and
integrity. In that spirit, we are proud to offer this book to our readers;
however, the story, the experiences, and the words are the author's alone.

To all members of our family

♥

Contents

Preface

As you read this book, I hope you'll feel like you're sitting with us, listening to Nana's stories. You might laugh, you might cry, but most of all, I hope you'll feel the love that flows through our family history.

I met someone so special, and she made the whole world brighter. That's my Nana, Carol Mavis Kent.

Being Nana Carol's first grandchild is really special. That means I get to be the one to tell you her story! When Grandpa (Ron) asked me to write a book about her, I felt a little nervous but also very excited.

You know how a butterfly starts out as this tiny caterpillar, and then goes through this amazing transformation? Well, that's kinda how I feel sitting here, about to share Nana Carol's story with you. Nana Carol had a way of making everyone feel important, and her life was full of love, adventure and hardships.

My Nana wrote her story in September 2001, and I helped finish it. It's a way for us to share her amazing life with you.

Nana's life wasn't always easy, but she was very strong and brave. I want to tell you about her because she taught me so much about love, family, and never giving up.

One of the most significant hardships in Nana's early years was the illness that struck her mother. Nana's mum, Mavis, fell gravely ill with diphtheria, a severe condition that left her bedridden and struggling to breathe. The prognosis was dire, with doctors doubting she would survive beyond her tenth year.

However, this challenging period demonstrated the strength that ran in their family. Against the odds, Nana's mother recovered, instilling in Nana a deep appreciation for resilience and the preciousness of life.

Mavis got better and grew up to be a strong woman. Her brother Vivian went away to WW1, and after he came home, he married Olive and they had a baby named Iris, who became my cousin.

Mavis later found love with a man named John. Together, they built a life filled with joy and warmth, welcoming my younger sister, Carmel Vivienne, and I into the world.

My Nana was all about love and accepting everyone. She supported everything we did. Whenever we brought friends or new people to meet her, she was always so happy and excited. She treated everyone the same, no matter who they were.

I remember how thrilled Nana was when my daughter,

Crystal, was born. Crystal was her first great-grandchild! But Nana was just as happy when all the other great-grandchildren came along, too. She had so much love to give.

One of my Nana's earliest memories was a long train ride from Perth to South Australia. She was only about three or four, and her sister was even younger.

The trip took four days and five nights! They had to sit up the whole time - no comfy beds for sleeping. At every stop, they met Aboriginal people and shared cookies with them. Even though they didn't have much, Nana's kindness shone through.

Their first home in South Australia was just one room. That's where they met Ted Hulbert, who later became their father. He was strict but also fun.

They moved to a house on Hutt Street, where they lived until Nana was about twelve. Every morning, they'd hear horses' hooves on the street and get visits from the milkman, iceman, and butcher.

Nana's mum hardly ever talked about her family when she was young. Maybe it's because they lived in Adelaide, while her relatives were way over in Perth. Or maybe she had bumpy relationships she wanted to forget. She didn't ask her enough questions either.

Nana really wishes she could go back and ask her mum all about her childhood. What were her parents and grandparents actually like? What amazing or difficult times did they live through? She'll never get those answers straight from her.

But my Nana can share the scattered pieces she does have.

It might not be the full picture, but it's her story from her side. She told it truthfully, holding nothing back - the good times, the bad, the honest thoughts and feelings too. Hopefully, it helps uncover who they really were.

This book is more than just a story - it's a way to remember and honour my Nana. Her life, with all its ups and downs, has shaped who I am today. By sharing her story, I hope to show you how important family history is and how the love and strength of one person can touch so many lives.

Nana wrote the first draft of this book, pouring her heart onto the pages. I've carefully edited it, adding my own thoughts and memories. It's been like having long talks with Nana, even though she's no longer here. Through her words, I've learned so much about our family and about life.

Thank you for joining us on this journey through time. Nana's life was full of challenges, but also full of love and strength. I hope her story inspires you to be brave, to be kind, and to cherish your own family stories.

So, as I start this book about her life, I invite you to get to know her too. She might not have been your Nana, but I bet by the end of this story, you'll wish she was. This is her story, told with truth and tenderness. Welcome to our family.

Karen Marie

CHAPTER 1

Tides of Time

When I was young, my mother kept her childhood memories locked up tighter than a safe. *Why does she hide everything? What could be so painful that she can't share?* I never got to discover the real her until it was too late. As I grew older, her silence about the past haunted me like a ghost. *Who were they, these mysterious people in her life before me? Who were her parents? What was her life like before me?* So many family secrets went untold.

Recently, my son Ted had a great idea. He suggested I write down whatever I can remember about my family story - the good and the bad. *Maybe this is my chance to finally understand.* To put together as much of the puzzle as I can.

For over a year now, I've been practising on the computer. At first, it was really fun learning new things. *Look at me, learning technology at my age!* But then I got a little bored. I didn't have enough actual tasks to do on it besides practice.

I couldn't let Ron know I was bored, though. *If he finds out, I'll be drowning in work.* If I did, he'd surely make me start writing a newsletter for Legacy (of which he volunteered) every few weeks! No way did I want more work like that. So instead, I started writing my family's history.

Mum hardly ever talked about her family when I was young. *Was she trying to protect us? Or protect herself?* Maybe it's because we lived in Adelaide, while her relatives were way over in Perth. Or maybe she had bumpy relationships she wanted to forget. We didn't ask her enough questions either.

Now I really wish I could go back and ask Mum all about her childhood. *If only I could turn back time, just for one conversation.* What were her parents and grandparents actually like? What amazing or difficult times did they live through? I'll never get those answers straight from her.

But I can share the scattered pieces I do have. *These fragments are all I have left of her.* It might not be the full picture, but it's our story from my side. I'll tell it truthfully, holding nothing back - the good times, the bad, the honest thoughts and feelings too. Hopefully, it helps uncover who we really were, at least a little.

Have you ever held a gold coin and felt its weight, its promise of a better life? *Dreams balanced on something so small, so fragile.* The whole town was built on that promise, where people gamble their dreams on specks of metal hidden in the earth. This isn't a fairy tale—it's where my story begins.

❁

My name is Carol Mavis Kent. My mother, Mavis Caroline Higgins, was born on March 20th, 1905, in a mining town called Boulder in Western Australia..

Her father, Charles Oswald Higgins, was a miner from Canada, and her mother, Caroline Higgins, a resilient woman, took care of my mother and her older brother Vivian after her marriage broke up when her children were very young. *Abandoned. Alone. How did she survive?*

Our family history is a story of strength and perseverance through difficult times. *Strength wasn't a choice—it was survival.* Can you imagine how hard it must have been for Caroline Higgins, raising two kids all alone, with no help from the government or anyone? *What silent tears did she cry when no one was watching?* There were probably many nights when my mum must have cried herself to sleep, feeling hungry and worried.

When she was just a little girl, she got very sick with diphtheria, a terrifying illness. *Death hovering so close, breathing down a child's neck.* Doctors didn't think she'd live past age ten. There weren't any vaccines back then to protect against such scary diseases, so families like ours lived in fear and didn't know what would happen next.

I get chills just thinking about poor mum lying in her bed, struggling to breathe and burning with fever. *My brave, fragile mother.* Nana Higgins must have been so scared she would lose her. *How does a mother watch her child nearly slip away?*

Somehow, my brave mother fought off the diphtheria. But it left her weak and sick for many more years. She had to do lots of her schooling from her bed at home. *Learning between breaths, between moments of pain.*

I imagine her feeling sad and left out, looking out the window, watching the other kids playing outside. So close, yet worlds apart. What I wouldn't give for a chance to go back and give her a big hug! Despite everything, my mother grew up into a strong woman. *Strength forged in suffering.*

Her brother Vivian went away to World War 1 and miraculously came back alive. Years later, he married Olive, and they had my cousin Iris.

My mum, Mavis Caroline, married my Dad, John Clifford Kent, when she was just 19. *So young, so vulnerable.* She was so young, like a flower still opening its petals. But their love didn't last. My Dad wasn't faithful, and it broke my mum's heart. *Love—fragile as glass, sharp as its broken edges.* I remember seeing sadness in her eyes, like rain clouds hiding the sun.

One day, something happened that made mum decide we needed to move to South Australia. *Another sudden change, another uprooted life.* She came home early and found a priest in our house.

My Dad's family, who were very Catholic, were trying to have Viv and me christened as Catholics without my mum knowing. *They were trying to claim us, erase her from our lives.* When she saw this, her face turned red like a sunset.

She was angry and felt like they were trying to take us away from her. *No one would steal her children, not after everything she'd been through.* "I won't let them control our lives," she told me later, her voice shaking.

My earliest memory is a long train ride from Perth to South Australia. *Four days trapped in a moving world, between what was and what might be.* I was about three or four years old, and my sister Viv was 18 months younger. The journey took four days and five nights!.

We sat up the whole time, no cosy beds for us. *Four endless days, how did we survive?* Mum was alone with two little kids. It must have been like herding butterflies, but she always said we were "very good children." *I glow with pride, even now, remembering her words.*

The train stopped often, moving slowly like a snail across Australia. At every stop, Aboriginal people met us. *Such a strange, wonderful parade of encounters.*

We gave them cream wafer biscuits and, strangely, newspapers. *Why newspapers? What stories were we sharing?* I still wonder why newspapers. *Did they read them? Use them for fires?* It's a puzzle piece that doesn't fit.

What amazes me most is Mum's kindness. *Even with nothing, she found something to give.* She barely had enough to feed us, her purse as light as a feather.

Yet, she bought biscuits to share. *A lesson bigger than any words.* It's like she was teaching us, "Even when life is hard, you can always give something." Her generosity was a seed planted in my heart, growing stronger each year.

This journey wasn't just across land. *It was a journey through emotions, through survival.* It was a trip through feelings—love for my grandfather, I wonder at Mum's strength, and about the people we met.

It was a long train journey, and even as a kid, I knew money was tight. *Every coin counted, every moment was a negotiation for survival.* I often wondered, "How did she pay for those train tickets?"

Family secrets are like buried treasure. *Some shine when brought to light, others cast long shadows.* Sometimes, digging them up brings joy. Other times, it brings questions.

When I close my eyes, I can still see the streets of my childhood in South Australia. *Each memory is a snapshot, fragile yet vivid.* Our first home in SA was a single room on North Terrace, right across from Royal Adelaide Hospital. The building was like a giant, two-story dollhouse. Now, I think nurses live there, or maybe it's fancy townhouses. We only stayed about a year, but that room I still remember.

There, Mum met Ted Hulbert (his full name was Albert Edward Hulbert). *Another chapter, another man entering our story.* He was like us, living in one room of that big house. Ted later became our stepfather. He was a retired English Royal Navy Officer who chose to live in Australia. He'd tell us spy stories, claiming he was in MI5. We'd listen, wide-eyed, but years later, we realised they were just make-believe—like the fairy tales Mum read us at bedtime.

From North Terrace, we all moved to 10 Hutt Street. *A new address, a new beginning.* This was home until I was about twelve. Back then, there were no big shopping centres. Instead, the shops came to us! *Our street was alive, a moving marketplace of daily necessities.*

Every morning, I'd wake to the clip-clop of horses. The milkman's cart would stop, and we'd run out with our billy can. He'd fill it from a big container, splashing some on his boots. *Such casual moments of connection.* Later, we'd leave empty bottles with money for full ones—much cleaner!

Next came the iceman, selling big blocks of ice that dripped on the footpath. But the most exciting was the butcher. His visit meant a slice of fritz for us and a bone for any dog around. *Small joys that made our world complete.* Those dogs would bury one bone, then dash back for another at the next house. Their tails wagged like crazy!

Eventually, the butcher stopped coming, so we'd walk to his shop daily. Without fridges, we couldn't keep meat fresh. But the rabbit man still came. *His cart was like a travelling promise of dinner.* His horse-drawn cart would rumble down the street as he called out, "Rabbit-oh!" For about 6 pence (5 cents today), he'd skin and clean a rabbit right there, his hands moving as fast as a magician.

Another regular was the Rawleighs man. *A travelling miracle worker.* His cart was like a travelling pharmacy. He had bottles of tablets that were supposed to cure everything from headaches to, well, anything that bothered you. There were ointments to rub on every part of your body, each promising to fix whatever was wrong. The funny thing is, they seemed to work! *Was it medicine or belief that healed us?* Maybe it was the belief that healed us, like a kind of magic.

Looking back, I see how much has changed. Today, we have huge stores with everything under one roof. But back then, our street was the store. Each day brought a parade of people, each selling one thing. It wasn't just shopping; it was a show, a community.

Every week, there was also the "Rag, Bones and Bottle" man on his horse-drawn cart. His sing-song voice echoed between the houses, "Rags, Bones and Bottles, any Rags, Bones or Bottles?" If you say it out loud, you'll hear the rhythm that used to fill our days.

Then there was the postman, coming twice a day, six days a week! *Communication was an event, not a constant.* He didn't sing; he blew a whistle when he left a letter. That whistle was like a dog alarm. Every pup in the neighbourhood would start a barking contest or try to snatch a piece of the poor postman's leg. I'd watch from behind the curtain, torn between worry for him and giggles at the chaos.

In some areas, there was even a "Night Cart." Now, this job wasn't glamorous. His task was to empty all the toilet waste buckets and leave clean ones. (No flush toilets back then!) *Imagine the dignity of such work.* I never lived where they used buckets, but I remember one holiday trip. We were driving behind a cart when a plastic bag fell off, breaking in front of our car. The smell! It was like all the world's stinky things in one spot. That memory still makes my nose wrinkle.

Those days were filled with excitement, but also with reminders of how little we had. *Poverty was our constant companion.* Our main shopping was on Rundle Street. There was a cake shop with cream cakes so beautiful they looked like jewels. *Desire trapped behind glass.* We could only afford to look, never to taste. The sight of those cakes, so close yet so far, taught me about longing.

Coles always advertised, "Nothing over 2 shillings and sixpence" (about 25 cents today). Even that was a stretch for us. On Fridays, we'd go to the East End markets for cheap fruits and veggies. *Survival required creativity.* They were usually bruised or second-grade, leftovers that couldn't be sold normally. But for us, those bruised apples and soft tomatoes were treasures. We didn't know any different.

When I think back, my heart squeezes. *Memory is both comfort and pain.* We weren't well off. The carts on our street—the ragman, the Rawleighs man—they were part of a world where every penny counted. Those cake shop windows reminded us of what we couldn't have. Yet, we found joy. *Happiness doesn't require wealth.*

The postman's whistle, the singsong calls, even the night cart's mishap—these moments sparkle in my memory..

I often wonder, "How did Mum and Dad keep food on our table?" *Survival was an art form.* It must have been a daily battle, like trying to fill a leaky bucket. But they did it. Their strength, their clever ways of stretching every cent, are the real treasures of my childhood.

Our home on Hutt Street felt like a cosy nest. *Safety in small spaces.* But school? That was a different story. My sister Viv and I went to Flinders Street Public School until grade seven. Then I moved on to Norwood Central Girls' School for a year, followed by Unley Central Girls' School. Back then, we were known as Kent—that was our last name. It wasn't until around 1944 or 1945 that we changed it to Hulbert.

I didn't like school much. *Learning felt like a battlefield.* Most subjects were like puzzles where I couldn't find the right pieces. Take dressmaking—oh, it was my worst! It was usually on Mondays, and like clockwork, I'd "forget" my sewing. *A small rebellion against expectations.* I'd have to trudge home, my cheeks burning with embarrassment, to fetch it. This trick made me miss most of the lessons.

Each unfinished dress or skirt was like a flag, signalling my struggle. But you know what? That's okay. We all have things we're not good at, just like we all have hidden talents waiting to be discovered.

In my second year of high school, shorthand class was where I excelled. *Finally, a language that made sense to me.* The squiggles and loops weren't just marks on paper; they were my secret language. I quickly rose to the top of the class, loving every swoosh of my pen. Geography was another bright spot. Maps weren't just paper; they were windows to far-off lands.

So, while school often felt like wading through mud, there

were moments when I found solid ground—even a few flowers. *Life is about finding your own path.* It taught me that we all shine in our own ways, sometimes in places we least expect.

❖

In our new home, we were like birds that had flown far from their nest. *What would Dad's family think of us now?* We lost touch with Dad's family. Once, during World War II, my cousin Kevin reached out. We wrote letters back and forth for a while, like sending paper boats across an ocean. "Dear Kevin," I would write, "Life here is different, but we're making do." But then, like so many things in my life, that connection drifted away.

Now, Iris is my only cousin that I know. She's like a steady lighthouse in my family's foggy history. She was married twice, first to Charles Gray, but when he passed away, she married Charles McLorinan. Today, she lives in a retirement village in Marangaroo, a suburb of Perth. We keep in touch, sharing stories and memories like treasures.

Recently, I was on the phone with my cousin Iris in Perth. As we talked, it was like opening an old, dusty diary. *Could she really know something about our past that I don't?*

"Your Nana Higgins organised it," she said, her voice crackling through the phone line. "She thought it would be better for your mum to get away from your birth father."

My heart skipped a beat—finally, a piece of the puzzle! *All these years, and Nana had been the one.*

Iris shared surprising information, including birth certificates, marriage papers, and a list of names. *Eleven siblings? How could we not have known?* Turns out, my Nana Higgins had eleven brothers and sisters! That means Mum had a whole garden of uncles and aunties. But she never talked about them. It's like they were flowers she kept hidden. Well, not all of them.

Years later, when I had my own kids—Lel, Glenda, and Nown—we visited Mum's aunt Ivy in Ipswich, Queensland. I remember her daughter, Dorothy, too. *Would my children understand the weight of this family reunion?* We even have a newspaper clipping about our visit, like a pressed flower in a book.

This memory makes me feel warm, like sunshine after rain. But it also makes me wonder, why didn't Mum talk about her big family? *Was she protecting us, or herself?* Was she protecting us, like a mother bird shielding her nest? Or was there sadness she wanted to forget?

The pages I have are filled with feelings—sadness, confusion, and sometimes anger. Yet, there's also love, especially for my mum and sister. *Some days, I wish I could go back and ask Mum all the questions I was too young to know to ask.*

We've been through a lot together, like travellers on a long journey. Even without knowing all the details, I cherish our story. It's uniquely ours, with all its twists and turns.

I tried to connect with my birth father, even though he'd been missing from my life for years. *What would I even say to a stranger who shared my blood?*

My sister Viv used to write letters to our uncle, who was a Catholic priest at a school in Melbourne. It was like sending messages in bottles, hoping they'd reach someone who knew our family's secrets. Through him, our Grandfather Kent, my father's father, found me.

"You should write to him," Grandfather Kent urged gently. "He's your father, after all."

But is he really? My heart whispered. *What makes a father - blood or love?*

I decided to be brave. I wrote a letter, starting with "Dear Father." As I wrote those words, my hand felt heavy. *How strange that two simple words could feel so foreign on the page.*

For years, we'd called another man "Father," someone who'd been there for us. Now, writing to my real father felt as strange as wearing someone else's shoes.

His reply left me feeling cold, like I'd stepped into a chilly stream. "Blood is thicker than water," he wrote. Those words stung. *Where was this precious blood when we needed new shoes for school?* Not a single birthday card or Christmas wish. Nothing for years. *Did he ever think of us on those special days?*

Now, as I look back, my heart softens a bit. I wonder if he did think of us during those times, sending silent wishes our way. *Perhaps there's more to his story that I'll never know.*

Maybe Mum kept his messages from us, trying to protect our hearts like a mother bird sheltering her chicks. But we'll never know, will we? It's like trying to catch smoke—impossible.

This experience taught me that family isn't just about blood.

It's about who's there when you need them, who warms your heart, and that's a lesson I'll always keep, like a treasure in my pocket.

Some memories are faded, but others are as bright as the day they happened. Years after trying to connect with my birth father, I kept writing to my Grandfather Kent.

"Come visit us," I wrote one day. "Come meet your great-grandchildren." *Would he see pieces of himself in their faces?*

One day, feeling brave and hopeful, I invited him to Adelaide. By then, I had three kids of my own. When he visited, it was like sunshine filling our home. He was a gentle, kind man with stories that made us laugh and think.

"These books," he'd say, running his fingers over the Braille translations he worked on, "they're like bridges to other worlds." I remember his hands, wrinkled like tree bark, which he used to translate books into Braille for blind people. He also volunteered in a Western Australian jail. His life was about helping others, like a lighthouse guiding ships through dark waters. When he passed away years later, it felt like losing a piece of our heart, losing a wise old tree from our family garden.

Looking back, I see how much has changed. These memories are like old photographs, a bit faded but full of life. The clip-clop of horses, the drip of ice, the excitement of a free slice of fritz—these sounds and feelings are part of me.

Some questions will always remain unanswered, I think to myself as I write these memories down. As I look back on my life, it feels like a book with some pages missing. But that's okay. Family secrets are like buried treasure. Sometimes, digging them up brings joy. Other times, it brings questions. But these fragments, however incomplete, are our story - and they deserve to be told. These memories are my treasure map, guiding me to understand who I am.

CHAPTER 2

The Heart of Hulbert's Shop

Our childhood days weren't perfect, but they were full of small joys that made hard times bearable. *Sometimes I wonder if anyone really understands how we survived those years.* Can you remember any small pleasures from your childhood?

In 1932, when I was eight years old, our weatherboard house on Hutt Street, Adelaide, stood as a testament to making do with less. *Another week of stretching every penny,* the Depression had wrapped its lean fingers around every family in our neighbourhood, but even then, we found ways to sweeten the bitter times. Every Friday evening, as the summer sun cast long shadows through our lace curtains, my sister Viv and I would press our faces against the window, watching for our stepfather Ted Hulbert's familiar silhouette. *He's coming, he's coming!*

The ritual began the same way each week. Ted, exhausted from his work but never too tired for this game, would slip something into the living room while we squeezed our eyes shut tight, giggling with anticipation. "Ready?" he'd call, and we'd scramble to begin our search, our bare feet pattering across the worn floorboards. *Where could it be this time?* Ted was lots of fun, but he was a little strict sometimes, like he didn't let my sister Viv and me have friends over to play.

The prize was always the same - a chocolate frog that seemed enormous to our child-sized hands, nearly twice the size of the ones you see today. *How does he always manage to find this treasure?* Back then, it cost just a penny, but to us, it might as well have been made of gold. *A whole penny! What luxury!* We never knew where Ted managed to find that spare penny each week, not when so many men couldn't find work at all.

Those Friday night searches became our anchor in a world where our parents whispered worriedly about bills after they thought we were asleep. *If they only knew how much we could hear, how much we understood.* Under the tank stand, behind Mum's sewing basket, tucked beside the wireless - the hiding spots changed, but the joy remained constant. Viv and I would split each frog with surgical precision, *carefully, so carefully - we must make this last,* savouring every sweet crumb, making the treat last as long as possible.

This is our rebellion against hard times. This was childhood in the Depression, where a penny chocolate frog could transform an ordinary Friday into a celebration, where the simple game of hide-and-seek with our stepfather could make us forget, if only for a moment, about the empty cupboards and the worn-out shoes that pinched our growing feet.

We never got allowances or pocket money. But if Mum sent us to the store, sometimes she'd surprise us with a halfpenny, just half a cent! *A halfpenny! My heart would leap at the sight of that tiny coin.* To us, that felt like striking gold. With that tiny coin, we could buy six jelly babies to share.

"Three for you, three for me," I'd say to Viv, dividing our treasure. Their sugary sweetness melted in our mouths as we savoured each bite.

Some of my most vivid memories are the smells of our modest snacks, like the yummy aroma of bread slathered with dripping (that's the solid fat from meat). We'd sprinkle salt and pepper on top. *That first bite - pure heaven!* Even today, when my sister Viv visits, she always hopes I have dripping so we can enjoy that delicious treat again.

"Remember how we used to eat this after school?" she'll say, her eyes twinkling with nostalgia. *And just like that, we're children again.*

Speaking of bread, I have a confession - there were times I couldn't resist taking a bite straight out of the fresh loaf on the walk home from the bakery! *The warm, yeasty smell was torture - how could anyone resist?* The doughy centre was just too tempting. Of course, I always blamed it on Viv. "Must've been Viv," I'd say innocently when Mum discovered the missing chunk. I loved my sister, but telling fibs was one of my flaws as a kid.

The rooms in our humble home on Hutt Street helped make ends meet. We rented out the two small upstairs rooms off the kitchen, the one tiny room off the back porch, and even three rooms inside the house itself. Money was that tight.

Ah, the inside bathroom - now that was an adventure! I can't recall if toilet paper existed yet, but we surely couldn't afford such a luxury. Instead, we relied on recycled newspaper squares strung together. *The rustle of those newspaper pages still echoes in my memory.* Hanging there on a nail, those makeshift supplies helped keep our little family clean. With so many people sharing the house, there was no privacy.

I remember many nights when Mum, Dad, my sister Viv, and I all squeezed into one bedroom. Viv and I slept on a mattress on the floor, but we didn't mind one bit. *In the dark, Viv would whisper, "Are you awake? Let's look at the presents!"* That's because we could have sneak peeks at our Christmas presents hiding under Mum and Dad's bed!

What simple treasures those humble gifts were - a new pencil case, an orange, and a handmade dress from Mum's talented hands. "Look what Santa brought!" we'd exclaim, knowing full well it was Mum who'd stayed up late sewing. Receiving them filled my heart with more joy than you could imagine. These days, kids expect endless toys and gadgets. But back then, any present at all felt like a world to us.

Perhaps that's why I've always tried to teach my own children and grandchildren the value of simple things. Those early lessons in gratitude shaped who I became - someone who finds joy in small pleasures and believes that love, not money, makes a house a home. Growing up with little taught me to appreciate everything, to waste nothing, and most importantly, to share what I have with others. Even now, when I give gifts to my grandchildren, I try to include something handmade, something that carries love in every stitch - just like Mum's dresses did for me.

Church played a big role in our young lives, too. We started out attending Sunday school at St. Paul's until the pastor made a comment that really irked Mum. "We won't be coming back," she declared firmly that day. From then on, we went to Flinders Street Baptist for all the usual activities— Sunday school, services, youth group, you name it. For a while, I even helped teach the little ones about God's love.

Sundays in our household were quiet affairs when I was a girl. Viv and I had one special weekly task - writing letters to our Nana Higgins, who lived far away in Perth. *The blank page would stare back at me as I struggled to find words.* My letters never contained much excitement, just simple updates like "I went to Sunday school today" or "School was good this week."

"What else should I write?" I'd ask Viv, chewing my pencil.

Filling even one page always felt like a struggle. With not much else allowed on the Lord's Day, Sundays felt rather boring to my restless kid mind. We couldn't sew, knit, or even play outside. *Hours stretched like taffy as we sat quietly, trying to be good.* Not exactly an action-packed childhood!

❁

Times were really tough when my baby brother Ted was born in 1934. It was right between the two World Wars, during the Depression years. *Every penny had to stretch until it screamed.*

Mum worked long hours as a seamstress, sewing clothes to earn money. Her needle would flash in the lamplight, *tick-tick-tick*, well into the night. Dad tried his best to find jobs, but work was almost impossible to find back then.

I'll never forget one heartbreaking time when Dad sold vacuum cleaners, going door-to-door. *Please, let someone buy from him today,* I'd pray each morning as he headed out. After walking the streets all day, he'd come home with bloody blisters on his poor feet from his ill-fitting shoes.

"Just need to rest them a bit," he'd say with forced cheerfulness, but I saw the pain in his eyes. The sight of him soaking his crushed toes in a dish of salt water still makes me flinch. *How many doors had slammed in his face that day?*

Despite the struggles, Mum's pregnancy brought a ray of hope into our lives. "Will it be a boy or a girl?" I'd wonder aloud, pressing my ear to Mum's growing belly. I couldn't wait to meet my new sibling! When Ted finally arrived, he was the most precious thing I'd ever seen. His chubby cheeks and curly blonde hair filled me with pure wonder and love.

Since our parents had to work relentlessly, the kind Bridgeman neighbours watched over Ted during the daytime.

Thank heaven for good neighbours. I still have fond memories of their backyard cow that provided fresh milk.

"Run along to school now," Mrs Bridgeman would say. "Your little brother's in good hands."

As soon as I got home from school, I happily took over babysitting duties from Mrs Bridgeman. Cradling my infant brother's warm little body, I felt like the luckiest big sister in the world. *His baby smell was sweeter than any perfume.*

In those lean years, moments of joy were hard to come by. But baby Ted's gurgles and giggles wrapped our home in a cosy blanket of peace. Gazing into his bright, trusting eyes, I glimpsed a future beyond the Depression's miseries. *Even on the darkest days, his smile was like sunshine.*

My brother represented hope, innocence, and the triumph of new life over tough circumstances. Holding him was like glimpsing a world made whole again after being shattered into pieces. *Maybe that's why I've always believed in new beginnings.*

Next door to the Bridgeman's lived the Clark family. I'll never forget the grandmother's funny last name - Bottomley! Their daughter Jean had to keep both legs in casts for years because of her deformed hips. *Poor Jean, trapped in those heavy casts while we played outside.* Little did I know that same house would become a special place for me much later in life.

Birthdays were simple but special when my sister Viv and I were little girls living on Hutt Street.

"Your turn for the big present this year!" Mum would announce with excitement. We took turns getting the "bigger" gift that year. If it were my birthday, I'd get the larger doll, and on Viv's big day, she'd receive the bigger one. *It seemed so fair then, so perfect.* Looking back, those loving traditions showed how creatively Mum and Dad tried to make everything fair between us, despite money being tight.

Some of my fondest memories are the delicious treats we made out back. When the small room off the verandah wasn't rented out, it became our little ice cream factory!

"Keep turning!" Mum would encourage us as our arms got tired. We'd carefully follow Mum's recipe, taking turns churning the sweet cream into a frozen dream. *The anticipation made it taste even better.* That first bite of our homemade ice cream is a flavour my taste buds will never forget.

The verandah wasn't just for fun and games, though. One day, Viv came racing out the front gate and smacked right into a steel light pole. *The sound still haunts my nightmares.* I'll never forget the sickly sound of her head splitting open, or the growing pool of blood on the pavement.

"Stay still, darling," the doctor soothed as he stitched her up right there on that verandah. The scar still remains, an unwanted reminder of childhood's bumps and scrapes.

We didn't have much money or fancy things in our lives. Instead, we had family, laughter, and cherished every little thing we had. *Rich in love, if not in pocket.* I wouldn't trade those warm memories from Hutt Street for anything.

When I turned twelve in 1936, everything changed. Mum and Dad opened our very own shop in St. Peter's, and we moved to a new house on Fifth Avenue. *Our very own shop – it felt like a dream!* I remember skipping down the street that first day, feeling so grown up because our family finally had a real business.

"Welcome to our shop!" I'd practice saying it in different voices. But oh, that shop! It was like a tin can sitting in the sun—all galvanised iron that sparkled and shimmered in the heat. I learned pretty quickly not to lean against those metal walls in summer. One touch and you'd jump back like you'd been bitten!

Sometimes I tell people about that summer of '36, and they can hardly believe it when I mention the temperature reached 120 degrees Fahrenheit. *You could have fried an egg on those iron walls.* But a child's memory doesn't lie about days that felt hot enough to melt your shoes.

"Ready for another day of battle with the heat?" Dad would joke each morning. He was clever about fighting the heat, though. Every morning, I'd help him set up what we called our "cooling system"—really just blocks of ice in bowls with fans pointed at them. *Our primitive air conditioning,* we'd laugh. I loved watching the ice slowly shrink, creating little rivers of water that we had to keep mopping up. The fans would whir away all day, pushing slightly less hot air around the shop while we all dripped with sweat.

My special job was watching the chocolate display. "Keep an eye on those bars," Dad would say with a wink. *Guardian of the chocolates – my first real responsibility!* I'd feel so important, monitoring them like a guard. Sometimes they'd start to slouch anyway, and we'd have to quickly shuffle everything around before we ended up with chocolate soup!

"Quick, Viv! Help me move these before they melt!" I'd call out in panic. *The great chocolate rescue happening almost daily in summer.*

The cash register became my best friend that summer. I'd stand on my tiptoes to reach it properly, loving the satisfying 'ding' it made when I rang up a sale. *Each 'ding' meant success – we were real shopkeepers!* Between customers, Mum would show me how to arrange the window display "just so," and I'd pretend our little shop was the fanciest store in all of Adelaide.

"A little to the left," she'd guide me. "Now that looks perfect." *Her praise made me feel ten feet tall.*

At home, we had to be just as creative about keeping things cool. While the shop had some kind of big industrial fridge for the ice cream and milk, our house had something much more interesting - our "cool safe." *Our very own miracle box,* I used to think. I thought it was the cleverest thing in the world! It looked like a cupboard wearing a damp hessian bag dress with wire mesh on the sides and a space on top to place a big block of ice like a hat.

No matter which cold-keeping invention we used, though, they all had one annoying flaw - the dripping! *Drip, drip, drip – the soundtrack of summer.* We'd have to carefully position a tray or dish underneath to catch the constant dribble of melted ice water. More often than not, we'd forget about emptying it until the tray overflowed, causing a mini-indoor monsoon. I'll never forget frantically sopping up puddles with towels, hoping Mum didn't notice.

"Did anyone check the drip tray?" Mum's voice would ring out. *Oh no, not again!* Usually, that question came right after I'd gotten absorbed in other activities and forgotten all about it. As the ice thawed, the cool water trickled down special grooves inside the chest's walls, giving our perishables an icy embrace. The wet mess was worth it, though, to enjoy simple treats like a crisp, frosty apple or chunk of cheddar cheese on a blazing summer day.

How far we've come, I think, sometimes when I open my modern refrigerator. Back then, it felt more like a fun game - figuring out how to outwit the relentless Australian heat. Those clever cold safes and ice chests were our beat-the-heat superheroes!

When we upgraded to a proper ice chest a few years later, I felt like we'd stepped into the future. "Look how fancy we are now!" Viv would joke. It looked more like a proper piece of furniture, though it still needed ice on top. I loved watching the water trickle down those special grooves inside - it was as though we had our own indoor waterfall, especially when we forgot about the drip tray again!

I don't know if the summers felt hotter back then or if it's just my imagination, but I have vivid memories of incredibly long stretches of sweltering days and nights. *The air was so thick you could swim through it.* The absolute worst part was trying to sleep on those boiling summer nights. Our bedroom behind the shop would get so hot, the air felt thick enough to cut with a knife.

"I can't take it anymore," Viv whispered one particularly sticky night. That's when we came up with our brilliant plan - we'd drag our blankets and pillows outside and sleep under the stars.

Those nights were magical. *The sky seemed closer somehow, as if we could reach up and touch the stars.* The grass would tickle through our blankets, and the night air would finally cool our sun-baked skin. Viv and I would lie there whispering and giggling, counting stars until our eyes got heavy.

"What do you think we'll sell tomorrow?" Viv would murmur sleepily.

"Oh, hundreds of ice creams," I'd reply, already half-dreaming. Sometimes we'd make up stories about the people who'd buy from our shop the next day, or plan what we'd do with our first million pounds (mostly involving ice cream).

I don't recall mosquitoes being much of a nuisance on those balmy nights, which seems strange looking back. *Nature's small mercy, perhaps?* Maybe they just couldn't survive the extreme dry heat? Or perhaps the gentle breeze kept them at bay. Either way, I have such fond memories of drifting off to sleep, gazing up at the magical night sky as I tried to count every last star. *In those moments, despite the heat and the hardships, life felt perfectly complete.*

When I turned 14, I was finally able to quit school and join Mum and Dad working at the shop full-time. *No more dreary arithmetic lessons!* No more teachers, no more textbooks - I was over the moon! Being able to learn hands-on business skills from my parents felt much more rewarding.

Our shop was sandwiched between a boot repair store on one side and a dressmaking shop on the other. The kind dressmaker, Mrs Goldsworthy, must have seen my curiosity, because she ended up hiring me as an apprentice!

"Would you like to learn to sew properly?" she asked one day. *My heart nearly burst with excitement!* I'll never forget the excitement of starting my first real career at such a young age.

Mrs Goldsworthy's shop became my second home. While we stitched away, Mary and I would breathlessly recount the latest fiction novels we'd read to pass the time between customers.

"And then what happened?" Mary would ask, pins held between her lips. *Our needles would fly faster with each dramatic plot twist.* Telling "serial" stories from one day to the next made the chapters come alive in new ways. Those lively storytelling sessions sparked my lifelong passion for reading and writing.

From sweltering backyard campouts to landing my first job, it's amazing how much opportunity and magic can blossom, even among life's most mundane moments. *Every day held the possibility of something wonderful.*

My childhood may not have been picture-perfect, but it was overflowing with laughter, resilience, and beautiful surprises around every corner.

In those days before television, we had to get creative with entertainment. One of my favourite pastimes was listening to the radio serials and plays. *The wireless set was our window to other worlds.*

It's hard to imagine now, but real actors would stand in front of microphones, using just their voices and sound effects to bring whole worlds to life!

"Shhh," I'd whisper to Ted when our favourite show came on. The creaking of a door, the clomping of horse hooves - they made those noises by cleverly using props. As I tuned in each week, their performances transported me to faraway lands and grand adventures. *In my mind's eye, those radio plays were as vivid as any movie.* I guess it didn't take much to amuse us back then. We were a pretty simple-minded bunch, easily dazzled by the magic of storytelling.

Around that time, I started tagging along with my work friends Mary and Iris to their Methodist church. A group of eight of us became inseparable, going everywhere together. *We thought we were so grown up, walking arm in arm down the street.*

Little did I know, one of the boys, Ken Townsend, secretly became my very first boyfriend! The trouble was, I was so shy that I could barely muster up the courage to speak to the poor guy for our entire 12-month "courtship."

What do you say to a boy? I'd wonder desperately. "Hello," was about all I could manage, my face burning red.

Some of my most vivid memories from that time are the lively Friday night strolls up and down Henley Beach Road.

It felt like stepping onto the set of an old movie - couples arm-in-arm, groups of friends meandering along, everyone stopping to socialise at the local malt shop. *The street hummed with youth and possibility.*

On one such evening, my friends and I crossed paths with two young fellows named Jim Fraser and Bill Andrew. *If only I'd known then how* important Bill would later become.

In the midst of those idyllic Friday nights, my little brother Ted provided some unintentional mischief and comic relief.

One afternoon, a neighbour burst into our shop, "Mrs Hulbert! Do you know what your Ted is up to?"

Ted was wandering up and down the street, popping into various shops and houses. When people asked what he was doing, he simply held up a little pad and asked them to "sign this"! *That was Ted - always full of surprises.* To this day, I'll never understand why, but everyone humoured him, scrawling their names without question.

"What in heaven's name were you collecting signatures for?" Mum asked later.

Ted just shrugged, "Just wanted to see if they would." *That was Ted all over - curious about everything.*

I can only imagine the confused look on my poor mother's face as she realised what her son had been up to!

We didn't seem to stay put in any of those shops for very long when I was a kid. *Moving again, always moving.* I'm not sure why we kept moving around so much. Maybe the stores just weren't successful enough.

We left Torrensville and landed at a new shop on Jetty Road in Brighton. It was owned by the Cunnew family, who also ran the picture theatre right next door! *A shop next to a theatre – how grand that seemed!* From that point on, everyone called our humble little store "Hulbert's Corner Shop."

Time went by, and eventually Mum and Dad were able to scrape together enough money to buy the corner shop for ourselves.

"It's really ours," Mum whispered, tears in her eyes. *After all those years of moving, we had a real home.* Finally, we had a real permanent home! I was around 15 years old, Viv was nearly 14, and little Ted was five and just starting at the local Brighton Primary School.

With me helping at the shop and Viv old enough to get her first job, she left school to work at this place in town called Vardon's.

"You'll never believe what I found in the phone book today," she'd announce at dinner. A big part of her tasks involved proofreading things before they went to the printers. Viv even had to read through the entire phone book, which was a lot smaller back then!

Her dramatic readings of typos always made even the longest day better. She'd come home each night regaling us with amusing anecdotes about some of the bizarre names and typos she came across. Those silly stories always left us doubled over with laughter.

Our humble corner shop may have seemed ordinary to

outsiders. But for our frugal family, finally owning that cramped little store represented years of hopes, dreams, and immense hard work finally paying off. *Every shelf, every counter was a piece of our dream come true.* Hulbert's became more than just a business - it was our hard-earned home at last.

After we settled into our little corner shop in Brighton, the daily commute to my dressmaking job back in Torrensville became too far. While it was only about 12 miles to the city centre, the train ride took a whopping 45 minutes each way!

Nowadays, that same trip flies by in half an hour. But in those days, jobs were hard to come by, so I counted myself lucky.

I landed a new position at a dressmaking factory in Adelaide called Thelma's. "It's not quite Mrs Goldsworthy's shop," I told Mum, "but it's honest work." It wasn't exactly a glamorous studio - more like an assembly line of stitching!

Each morning, I'd find a stack of pre-cut dress pieces waiting at my work station, all rolled up like fabric burritos. *Another day, another dozen dresses.* My task was to carefully unravel one, sew my assigned portion of the dress, then roll it back up and pass it along to the next seamstress's station.

On and on the line would go, with each worker adding their unique stitch to transform those humble fabric rolls into vibrantly patterned garments..

By day's end, my fingers were calloused and my shoulders ached from hunching over yards of fabric. But I took immense pride in being a tiny cog in that giant dressmaking machine!

For my dedicated labour, I earned the princely sum of

seven shillings and sixpence each week - roughly 75 cents in today's currency.

"A penny saved is a penny earned," Mum would remind me. *Her voice echoed in my head every time I opened my coin purse.* While that may not seem like much now, I had to carefully budget every hard-earned penny. A portion went to pay for my room and board at home. Some was faithfully donated each Sunday at church. Any leftover scraps went into my savings, just as Mum always instructed.

Still, I always made sure to set aside one cherished penny for a very special treat - an ice cream on my long commute home from the factory! *That single penny bought a moment of pure joy.* I'd wait until the train rolled into Brighton station, then quickly dash off to the platform vendor.

There it was, my reward glistening in the late afternoon sun - a modest scoop of icy sweetness cradled in a crunchy cone.

"The usual, miss?" the vendor would ask with a knowing smile.

As I slowly savoured that penny lick, I'd replay the day's labour of love in my mind. Every back-aching stitch, every needle prick, every snipped thread - it all felt worthwhile. Because in that single, sugary indulgence, I tasted the sweet satisfaction of an honest day's work.

When World War II began in 1939, I was just 15 years old and working at Thelma's dressmaking factory. Suddenly, everything changed. Our assembly line got reassigned to important war work instead of fashionable frocks.

"We're doing our bit for the boys overseas," our supervisor

would say. From then on, my days were spent stitching scratchy wool berets for soldiers, piecing together sturdy ammunition bags, and sewing other military supplies I can't quite recall now.

The colourful cotton prints and delicate lace were replaced by drab olive greens and browns. *Every stitch felt like a prayer for victory.* But we didn't mind - we took pride in contributing to the war effort in our own small way.

Back at Hulbert's Corner Shop, the war's arrival meant my whole family was busier than ever before. Since our humble store sat right next door to the local picture theatre, it became our job to handle the Saturday night ticket queues.

"Quick, Viv! Another rush coming!" I'd call out. All day long, Mum, Dad, Viv, and I would take turns juggling the shop counter while also dashing back and forth to the theatre box office window.

When the evening movies let out for intermission, we'd frantically try to serve all the hungry patrons crowding our shop for snacks and refreshments. *The bell above the door jingled nonstop.*

"Two ice creams and a packet of Jaffas!" "Hurry, before the picture starts again!" *The voices would blur together in the rush.*

If the theatre was short-staffed any night, Viv and I would be whisked away from our shop duties to help usher guests to their seats.

Those non-stop evenings were a dizzying blur of ringing registers, splashing soda fountain drinks, and scrambling to restock candy boxes. By the time we locked up for the night, our feet throbbed and our voices were hoarse from calling out,

"Next! Who's next?"

As exhausting as that nonstop hustle was, I look back on it with immense fondness now. *In the darkest of times, our little shop glowed with life.* Our corner shop became the heartbeat of the neighbourhood during those war years—a place for neighbours to gather, share stories, and find moments of lightness during the heaviest times.

While the world wavered under war's dark cloud, our family's shop glowed like a living room's welcoming hearth.

Most significant of all, those relentless evenings working side-by-side cemented my bond with Mum, Dad and Viv like steel. *We were more than family - we were a team.* Our social lives were non-existent, sure. But we gained something far more precious - cherished memories of laughter, teamwork and tightly-knit togetherness in the most extraordinary circumstances.

CHAPTER 3

From Hardships to Dream

Ron's great-grandfather, Job Clark, was born way back in the 1800s in a tiny town called Beachport in South Australia. *A time so distant, yet its echoes still shape us.* When Job was just 23 years old, he married his sweetheart, Elizabeth. Together, they had a full dozen kids - can you imagine trying to feed and clothe a full dozen mouths as humble farmers? *The strength they must have had, the sacrifices they must have made.*

One of those 11 children grew up to be Ron's Dad, Alfred, though everyone called him "Stumpy." *A nickname that spoke of both affection and character.* Stumpy was born in the mining town of Broken Hill but later moved to Kalangadoo as a teenager. Feeling restless, he soon enlisted in the Boer War, where he became mates with some soldiers from Victoria.

"Adventure calls," he must have thought. After returning home unscathed from that first war, Stumpy realised he hadn't scratched his adventuring itch yet. So, he headed all the way back to South Africa, this time joining the Randell boys to seek his fortune in the gold mines!

Eventually, World War I called Stumpy back to defend his homeland. *From one battlefield to another, duty always calling.* This time, he fought in the Middle East and on the bloody Western Front, rising to the rank of Sergeant despite being wounded twice. He also sadly suffered exposure to those terrifying new chemical weapons.

When the Great War ended, Stumpy was given his own parcel of land near Kalangadoo as a reward for his service. *A soldier's payment in soil and sky.* It was there that he settled down, married a local girl named Ada May Caldwell, and finally traded his wandering ways for a peaceful life toiling the soil and raising a family.

Although Ada May Caldwell had grown up the daughter of a miner, life took an abrupt turn when she married Stumpy Clark and suddenly found herself a farmer's wife. *How strange it must have felt, trading lamp-lit tunnels for open fields.* Navigating that radical shift from her gritty miner's kid roots to tending a rural homestead couldn't have been easy.

From what I've heard, those first years on Stumpy's soldier settlement block at Weepar tested Ada's spirit. As a delicate, tiny-framed woman, the physical tolls of farm labour must have felt overwhelming at times. *Did she ever long for her old life?* I can vividly picture Ada's slender arms straining under the weight of heavy buckets brimming with freshly-skinned rabbits, even while pregnant with one of her five children.

"You'll learn, dear," the Kalangadoo women would say. The local ladies embraced the newcomer Ada with open arms, tutoring her in everything from mucking stalls to mending fences. While their nurturing guidance helped Ada master the backbreaking farm chores, she still faced a harsh reckoning - this life couldn't have been further from the world she knew as a young lass.

Four of Ada's five babies with Stumpy were born in the city of Mt. Gambier during those first years—Alfred Laurence in 1920, Sarah Wilmot in 1922, Wallace James in 1923, and the youngest, my future husband Ronald Edwin, in 1925. *Each birth was a reminder of the city life she'd left behind.* I often wonder if Ada's heart ached for her return to a more civilised, urbane existence with each new child's arrival.

Fate soon intervened when Stumpy's health began failing just months after Ron's birth. *The war's poison finally catching up.* With two little ones already of school age, a move from the isolated settlement into the township of Kalangadoo was arranged.

From what I understand, in those final years, various military veteran organisations helped facilitate the family's transfer from the settlement block to a War Service home in Edwardstown. This allowed Stumpy to be closer to proper medical facilities as his condition worsened.

✿

When Alf first got sick, he couldn't go home on the weekends like he used to. *Another empty chair at the dinner table.* His illness could spread to my family, so a little room was made up in the shed.

"We've made it nice and comfortable for you," Ada would say, her voice steady despite her worry. It must've felt weird sleeping out there instead of his real bed, but he was just happy to be out of the hospital for a bit.

He had to use special plates and cups that were just for him. *Each meal was a reminder of his separation.* He couldn't share with his family. It made him feel a little lonely and different, like he didn't belong.

But Ada would bring him snacks and tuck him in at night with an extra quilt to stay cosy. "Sleep well, my darling," she'd whisper through the door. *Her love reaching across the distance they had to keep.*

During that time, baby Betty was born in June 1929. *New life blooming even in the shadow of illness.* They were so excited for a new sibling!

But Alf couldn't hold her or be too close. *The cruellest part of his isolation.* He just peeked through the window to see her tiny face. "She has your smile," Ada would tell him, trying to bridge the gap between father and daughter.

Sadly, Ron's Dad, Alf, passed away in 1931. *The final goodbye stolen by circumstance.* He felt heartbroken that he missed saying goodbye. He was buried at the West Terrace Cemetery in the War Graves section; *another soldier's journey ended.*

After Ron's Dad died, his mum, Ada, got really sick too. *Grief can break even the strongest spirit.*

With no one to take care of the kids, they got sent to the Morialta Children's Home for nine whole months! *Nine months that felt like nine years.* They must've been scared being away from Mum, even though the people there were nice.

The Edwardstown RSL and Legacy groups helped look after Laurie, who was the oldest brother, since he was too old for the home. "Your father served his country," they'd say, "now we'll serve his family." *The brotherhood of soldiers extending beyond the grave.*

And our church, Edwardstown Baptist, pitched in to help Ada, too - like bringing her firewood in winter. *Small kindnesses that meant everything.* Back then, you couldn't get government help like today.

Once they were all back home, brothers Laurie and Ron went to the Goodwood Technical School to learn hands-on skills. *Together again, but changed by their time apart.* Wilma and Betty went to Unley Central, and Wally went to Unley High. It must've felt unfair to be separated like that just because of how smart you were.

After school, Ron got jobs as a film inspector and projectionist at the old Theatre Royal downtown. *Finding his own path in the world at last.*

Ada must've felt proud of him working at such an exciting

place! She had always dreamed of having an interesting career like that, too. "My boy at the Theatre Royal," she'd tell the neighbours, her voice warm with pride.

Those were some really tough years, being shuffled between hospitals, homes, and schools. *But love has a way of holding on.* But they stuck together as a family through it all. *Each hardship endured made their bonds stronger, each made their reunions sweeter.*

❈

When World War II started in 1939, everything changed for my future husband Ron's family. *Another generation called to war.* His oldest brother, Laurie, joined the Air Force, and soon after, his other brother, Wally, signed up for the Army too.

"I should be going too," Ron would say, frustration in his voice. He really wanted to enlist in the Army as well. But since his father had passed away and Laurie and Wally were already serving, the military decided Ron needed to stay home with his Mum. *The burden of being the last son at home.* Instead of the Army, they made him work at the Rubber Mills factory on South Road in Edwardstown, where the Bridgestone tyre place is now located.

Ron got a part-time job at the Colonel Light Gardens movie theatre in the evenings and on Saturdays. *At least the theatre brought some glamour to wartime life.* His job was to run the projector and show films to the troops coming back from the Middle East war. I remember him telling me he started out as just a "lolly boy" selling candy and ice cream in the theatre before working up to the projectionist role.

"That's probably where he met all his old girlfriends," his Mum would tease, eyes twinkling. *If only she knew I'd be the last one.* And she was right - Ron always had a lot of girlfriends back then! One of those old flames was a girl named Betty Lang. We actually ran into her years later - she had gotten married and her last name was Bollenhagen. She ended up being the mother-in-law to Ron's sister Julie! *Life has such funny ways of connecting the dots.*

When I turned 17 in 1941, I took a position at the Penfield munitions factory in Salisbury, now called Weapons Research. *From sewing dresses to building bombs - what a change.* My days were spent working long, tiresome shifts assembling artillery shells and other ammunition. The deafening machinery noises and pungent smells of gunpowder and metal still vividly haunt my senses all these years later.

"Every shell helps bring our boys home," the supervisor would say. *Each one a prayer for peace.* While that gruelling factory work wasn't exactly what a young, dreamy-eyed girl envisioned for herself, I felt proud to be contributing to our nation's defence.

After a couple of years at Penfields, something inside me yearned for more - I wanted to chase my lifelong passion for fashion and open my own little dressmaking shop! *Dreams don't wait for peace.*

So at nineteen years old, I took a huge leap of faith and

leased a storefront right on Jetty Road in Brighton. "You're mad to start a business during wartime," some said. *But when else do you need dreams the most?* Running that tiny boutique while still helping at Hulbert's Corner Shop and the picture theatre next door made for endless blurs of 18-hour workdays. But I've never been one to shy from a challenge.

Ron loved tinkering with engines, so his cars and bikes were always getting fixed up in his free time. *The eternal mechanic, always covered in grease.* He'd come pick me up on Sundays, still covered in grease from working on his latest project.

"Ronald Clark! Couldn't you have cleaned up first?" Dad would sputter. *Poor Dad, always trying to maintain proper standards.* But what was the point? We'd just be heading right back to Ron's mum's place for more work anyway.

Speaking of Ron's mum, those Sunday evenings at her house were always nice. *The warmth of family wrapping around us like a quilt.* We'd have tea, then walk over to the Edwardstown Baptist Church, where his mum and sister Betty sang in the choir.

"Come on, give it a try," Betty encouraged when they wanted me to join. They even tried getting me to sing a duet with Betty once. But I just froze up when it was my turn - not a single note came out! *Stage fright turning my voice to stone.* Betty had to sing it as a solo. I never worked up the courage to try choir again after that.

Ron's mum liked to save money by cooking over a wood stove in the winter instead of using the gas oven. In the evenings, we'd all cosy up around that wood stove, sticking our feet inside the open oven door to stay warm. Sometimes she'd have a fire going in the living room, too, but wood could be expensive. So, we'd just huddle together in that toasty kitchen most nights, watching the flames dance through the stove's little window.

"Scoot over and make room," Ron would say, squeezing in beside me. *Those simple moments of togetherness meant everything.*

Ron and I loved spending time with his sister, Wilma, and her husband Bill's kids, Valmai and Billy. *Such precious little ones.* They were such cuties, around 2 and 3 years old back then. Whenever we could, we would take them out for little adventures.

One day, we got a really fun idea. A chance to give something special. We convinced Wilma to dress Valmai and Billy up in their absolute best outfits.

"Just trust us," we told her with mysterious smiles. Then we surprised her and Bill by taking the kids into town to get their pictures taken at a real photography studio!

Oh, those precious little faces! Valmai looked like a princess in her frilly dress. And Billy was so handsome in his little suit. Getting those professional photos taken was something Wilma and Bill could never afford on their own. So, we wanted to give them that special memory.

When the photos came back, they were just beautiful. "Oh my goodness," Wilma whispered, tears in her eyes. *Some gifts mean more than money can measure.* I'll never forget the huge smiles on Valmai and Billy's faces in those pictures.

It was during this bustling season of my life that I first

locked eyes with the dashing young man who would eventually become my husband - Ron Clark. *My heart knew before my mind did.* An assistant projectionist at our local cinema, Ron would shyly slip into my boutique between movie reels, purchasing tea and sneaking sidelong glances in my direction.

"Another cup of tea?" I'd ask, pretending not to notice his blush.

Everything changed the night of June 6th, 1944 - D-Day. *A night of destiny in more ways than one.* Viv and I had attended a church dance that evening, and Ron was there too. We spent the whole enchanted night twirling across the dancefloor together, frozen in time.

"May I have this dance?" he'd asked. *And every dance after.*

As the final notes played, he gratefully planted our first teenage kiss on my lips. *The world stopped spinning for just a moment.* In that singular, trembling moment, I knew I'd met the partner I wanted laughing beside me through all of life's adventures.

My Dad took an instant dislike to Ron from the moment we started courting. *Why couldn't he see what I saw?* Whenever Ron would step into our corner shop, Dad would just huff away without a word. Instead of letting Ron enjoy his tea breaks at the theatre, we started secretly meeting up on the beach to spend time together.

Rain or shine, you could find the two of us huddled under the jetty, sipping our drinks and stealing shy glances. "Our own little world," Ron would say. *Those stolen moments became my tiny oasis away from Dad's disapproving scowls.*

As Ron and I grew more serious, I realised the only way to escape the tensions at home was to leave the nest. *Freedom called like a siren song.* I decided to join the Army, not just for patriotism, but for independence too.

"You're too young," Dad declared firmly. Unfortunately, he refused to grant his permission since I was underage. He wouldn't budge, no matter how I pleaded and reasoned. Finally, in April 1945, at age twenty, I defied Dad's wishes and enlisted in the Navy as a Stewardess instead.

Around that same time, my sister Viv and I officially changed our last name to Hulbert through a deed poll. *A new name for a new chapter.* While just a few words on paper, it felt like taking powerful first steps into the woman I dreamed of becoming - independent, strong-willed, and in full control of my own destiny.

My time in the Navy wasn't all that I'd dreamed of. *Every mile felt like a thousand.* More than anything, I terribly missed being near my fiancé, Ron, back in Adelaide. The loneliness felt suffocating at times.

"Just a few more months," I'd tell myself each night.

In October 1945, I faced a tough choice - either remain enlisted but station at the HMAS Torrens camp in Port Adelaide or accept my discharge papers. *The streets of Port Adelaide held shadows I didn't want to face alone.* I knew it wasn't the safest neighbourhood, and the thought of having to travel there alone at night filled me with dread.

So I decided my heart wouldn't allow me to be separated

from Ron any longer. *Love won out over duty.* I put in for an honourable discharge from the Navy that month. While it meant walking away from my duties, at least I could return home to the one I loved most.

One of my most cherished memories from my brief Navy stint in Melbourne was making lovely connections with Ron's cousin Rene Hands and her big, boisterous family. *A port in the storm, that's what they were to me.* Rene's brood included her husband Garn and five lively kids - Ian, Lance, Joy, Margaret, and little David.

"There's always room for one more!" Rene would say. Whenever I had a free weekend pass, Rene's warm hugs and homemade feasts awaited. She treated me and any Navy pals I brought along like one of her own. *The comfort of family, even far from home.* Those cosy weekends provided such a nurturing escape from the harsh realities of service life.

Our love story was just beginning, filled with adventure, challenges, and an unbreakable connection that would last a lifetime. *Sometimes the heart knows best what the future holds.*

CHAPTER 4

A Legacy of Love

When I think of it now, those early days of falling in love were caught up in the pulse of wartime Australia. *Every goodbye could have been our last.* Ron and I lived by the clock, with him always running to catch that next train. Back then, every moment felt like it might be our last. We were young and in love, but the war made us count each minute we had together.

"Just five more minutes," Ron would plead, though we both knew the train wouldn't wait. *Time was never on our side.*

Have you ever had to walk home in the pouring rain because you missed your ride? That's exactly what happened to Ron one night after visiting me. After the pictures had ended at Brighton, Ron would come over to our house. We'd sit on the side verandah to say goodnight as he waited for his train to

Edwardstown. *Those precious moments of twilight togetherness.*

"The train can wait one more minute," he'd whisper. He frequently had to run to catch it, but one night he missed it completely and had to walk all the way home. Oh, his mother was so mad!

"That girl is nothing but trouble!" she'd declared. *Her words stung, but our hearts knew better.* She didn't sugarcoat it - to say she was cross was an understatement. Her biggest gripe wasn't even with Ron, though. She blamed me for "leading him astray" since I was older. That moment sticks in my memory - not just for the drama it caused, but because it was the first time I realised how our age difference might shape our relationship. Little did his mother know, her disapproval only strengthened our determination to be together. *And oh, if she only knew half of Ron's adventures!* Little did she know, Ron didn't need my help getting into mischief!

Around this time, my brother Ted was about 10 years old. *Still so young and full of curiosity.* He spent a lot of time helping in our shop, but he was still in school with homework and sports activities. Ted went to Brighton Primary and then Brighton High after 7th grade. He loved spending time at the beach too, probably more than Viv and I did.

"Look what I made!" he'd exclaim proudly. Ted was really into making and fixing radios - he even built a little crystal set, which was a common project for boys back in those days. *His clever hands always tinkering with something.* Later, around 18, Ted joined the Air Force to do his National Service.

The war had touched everything in those days, even our simple motorcycle rides. *The thrill of danger mixed with young love.* Looking back, I can still feel the wind in my hair and the excitement in my heart as we navigated around fallen trees and power lines. Youth made us fearless - perhaps too fearless.

The day I finally met Ron's brother, Wally, was unforgettable - and not in a good way! Ron picked me up from Brighton on his motorcycle. "Hold on tight!" he shouted over the storm. The weather was atrocious, with pounding rain, hail, and howling winds. Trees and power lines had toppled over on South Road, and we had to carefully weave our way through the debris. *Each crack of thunder made my heart jump.* My heart pounded with fear, but meeting the family favourite, Wally, made it all worthwhile.

"So this is the girl who's been keeping Ron out late!" Wally had teased warmly.

Wally had an amazing singing voice and joined the church choir along with a group called the "Glee Club." *His voice could lift spirits even on the darkest days.* Some of his good friends over the years were Ron Vick, also a talented singer, and Dave Rivett. We still see them around occasionally. There was also a chap named Charlie Baker who has since passed away.

Back then, Ron worked behind the scenes at the old Theatre Royal on Hindley Street. One Sunday, he invited the entire cast of the current show to join us on a bike ride out to Waterfall Gully. "The more the merrier!" he'd declared. *What an adventure that was!* I'll never forget pedalling all the way from Brighton to meet Ron in Edwardstown, then continuing on together with the whole theatrical troupe!

When I turned 21 in 1946, Ron was still only 19, almost 20 that December. *Age seemed such a small thing compared to love.* That age gap that had so worried Ron's mother now seemed insignificant in the face of all we'd shared. We had my birthday party at the R.S.L. Hall in Hove, where my father was a member. The R.S.L. Hall held special meaning for us - it was where so many families gathered to support each other during the war years, where news was shared and comfort found.

"We'll make it beautiful," Mum had promised. It seemed fitting that it would host this milestone in my life. Mum, my sister Viv, and I did most of the cooking and setting up for about 120 people, with a little help from friends like Mrs Crowhurst.

Even feeling unwell, I was determined to make it special. I made a special floral dress just for the occasion and one for Viv too - same pretty pattern but in slightly different colours. Growing up, Viv and I always got the same things, one after the other. Have you ever had to do something you really didn't enjoy, especially when you weren't feeling your best? That's how I felt that day, but we didn't talk about certain female things back then. *Some discomforts had to be borne in silence.*

❈

With Ron's brothers Laurie and Wally both back home from the war, Ron was finally able to enlist, too. But when he went to the recruiting office, they suggested we get married first, since we were planning on it anyway.

"Three weeks," they told us. *My heart nearly stopped.* We only had 3 weeks to get everything ready!

Three weeks to plan a wedding might seem impossible now, but in 1946, we were used to making do and acting quickly. *The war had taught us not to wait for perfect moments.* The war had taught us that tomorrow wasn't guaranteed - when happiness presented itself, you grabbed it with both hands.

Those three weeks tested every skill I had learned growing up in a resourceful family. *My fingers flew over the sewing machine like never before.* In those 3 weeks, I made our wedding cake (a friend decorated it), my cream-coloured wedding dress out of matalase crepe material, and Viv's blue bridesmaid dress in the same fabric with fancy trim at the waist.

"You're miracle worker," Mum would say, watching me work. *Every stitch had to be perfect.* I even sewed my going-away suit from brown pinstripe material, arranged the flowers, and hired a photographer. A friend loaned me a gorgeous, long lace veil.

We sent out 120 invitations and had the reception at the Hove R.S.L. hall. Ron and I got married that Friday night, March 22nd, 1946, at the Brighton Baptist Church. *Friday weddings weren't common, but the shop came first.* It had to be a Friday since the shop needed to be open on Saturdays.

I started my wedding day feeling sick to my stomach from nerves and excitement. *Of all days for nature's timing!* Back then, that was pretty normal for me during "that" time of the month.

So, Viv, Ron, Laurie, and Wally did most of the work decorating the church with ribbons and flowers since I wasn't feeling well.

"You rest, we've got this," Viv insisted, shooing me away from the decorations.

Laurie was our Best Man, Viv the Bridesmaid, and Wally sang "I'll Walk Beside You" during the ceremony. *His voice filled the church like a blessing.* The minister was Reverend Parrott from the Edwardstown Baptist Church. We were running a little late to the photographer, and he was already trying to close up for the night - not happy about having to stay open for us!

There were two reasons we were late getting to the photographer. First, since the minister was a friend of ours, he made his words extra-long during the service. *Every word seemed to last an eternity!*

Secondly, as we came out of the church, "Look out!" someone shouted, but too late. *So much for our grand exit!* Ron tripped over the camera wires and equipment belonging to the person who was supposed to film us outside! We never did get any of those outside videos.

We did take some professional photos inside, though even that was a challenge. *The photographer's patience wore thinner by the minute.* The photographer seemed quite grumpy and had particular trouble arranging my long lace veil in the camera frame.

"A little to the left... no, right... no..." he muttered endlessly. It must have been a bad day for that poor photographer!

Our reception was held at the R.S.L. Hall in Hove. I don't remember who catered the food; maybe it was the R.S.L. ladies or the C.W.A. group. But I'm pretty sure everyone had a great time celebrating with us. Ron and the minister certainly did - a little too much even!

"Just one more toast!" Ron would say, leading the minister away. *Oh, those men and their celebrations!* Ron kept taking the minister out to the back room with the R.S.L. members and giving him extra sips of their drinks.

The minister got a bit too merry and started entertaining us all with silly jokes. "And then the penguin said..." he'd begin, barely able to finish for laughing. *Some of those jokes weren't quite suitable for a wedding!*

Ron and I spent our wedding night at the South Australian Hotel on North Terrace, right across from Parliament House. No one knew where we were staying - it was a surprise. *This isn't quite the fairytale setting I dreamed of as a girl,* I thought as we entered our room, *but somehow it feels just right for us.* Our wedding night wasn't the romantic dream young girls imagine, but it was perfectly us - making the best of circumstances, finding humour in discomfort, and facing challenges together. The room was tiny and stuffy since it was a hot night with no air conditioning.

"Well, this is cosy," Ron said with a wry smile as we surveyed our quarters. We could open the window, but there was just a brick wall a few feet outside, blocking any breeze.

The next morning, we set off for our honeymoon. Before the wedding, we had secretly sent our luggage ahead to the Vine Inn hotel in Nuriootpa. I gave my suitcase to my brother Ted to put on the train at the Brighton station. *Surely Ted will handle this simple task,* I remember thinking confidently. Ron took care of his own bags, which was a good thing since I messed up on mine!

Back then, you needed special travel permits because of shortages from the war. We even had to get petrol coupons for the trip to Nuriootpa. *Another reminder that we're starting our marriage in unusual times,* I thought. When we arrived at the station, a car with a huge gas producer trailer picked us up and drove us to the hotel.

But there was another problem waiting - the porter could only find Ron's luggage! "We have one case for Mr Clark," the porter announced, "but nothing for Mrs Clark." *Oh no!,* I thought, my heart sinking. There was a single bag for a "Miss Hulbert" instead. In those days, unmarried couples didn't travel together like that.

"You see," I explained, feeling my cheeks flush, "I just got married yesterday..." The hotel staff's expressions softened as they realised we were newlyweds after the mix-up.

Our honeymoon at the Vine Inn was special, but not without its awkward moments. The first day was scorching hot, and Ron and I were relaxing on the bed, reading. Suddenly, there was a knock, and before we could say "come in," two cleaners barged through the door.

"Oh!" I gasped, trying to cover myself in my petticoat while Ron scrambled for his shirt.

"We need to change the bedspread," one of the cleaners

announced matter-of-factly, seemingly oblivious to our embarrassment.

Another time, we went on a tour to Seppelts Winery. *I wish I could understand a word this fellow is saying,* I thought as our toothless guide slurred through his increasingly wine-influenced explanations. Despite these funny incidents, the Vine Inn holds a special place in our hearts.

After the honeymoon ended, Ron had to report for Army duty. At the Adelaide Railway Station, I bid him farewell as he boarded a troop train to the recruit camp in Greta, New South Wales. "I'll write every chance I get," he promised, giving my hand one final squeeze. *Be brave,* I told myself, *don't cry until the train leaves.* The journey took almost a week because the train was frequently shunted into sidings to let other trains pass. The Adelaide Railway Station platform where I bid Ron farewell marked the true beginning of our marriage - learning to be together even when apart. As I watched his train disappear, I understood that marriage in wartime meant sharing your love with duty to country.

After just three months of training at Greta, Ron was sent for further training with the cinema unit in Sydney. *At least he's still in Australia,* I consoled myself. He stayed at the Pontiac Motor Pavilion H.Q. Trade Centre at Victoria Barracks, Paddington, for a few weeks. Then, he was posted as a replacement projectionist at the Cowra Prisoner of War and Internee camp.

Around September or October 1946, I made up my mind

to join Ron in Cowra. *We've been apart long enough*, I thought firmly. "Are you sure you want to make that journey alone?" my mother asked. "I'll manage," I assured her, though I wasn't entirely confident myself.

I travelled all the way from Adelaide by myself. First, I took the "Aurora" train to Melbourne, which wasn't too bad. But the journey from Melbourne to Cowra was dreadful! *Of all the seats on this entire train,* I thought miserably, *why did I have to end up next to the toilet?* The train was dirty, and the lavatory smelled awful.

Somewhere along the way, around 2 am, I had to change trains. "Four more hours until the next train," the station master informed me. *Just keep thinking about seeing Ron,* I told myself as I waited in the chilly pre-dawn hours until 6 am for the connecting one.

When I finally joined Ron in Cowra, he had rented a single room in a boarding house for me to stay. It was about 2 or 3 kilometres away from the camp where he worked as a projectionist. "It's not much," Ron said apologetically as he showed me the room, "but it's the best I could find." *It's perfect,* I thought, *because it means we're together again, even if only sometimes.* Ron could only stay with me some nights and weekends when he got leave.

"You won't believe how quick I can get here," he boasted one day. "Watch me run over those hills - just four minutes flat!" *My husband, the athlete,* I thought with amusement, watching him sprint away across the landscape. Those brief moments together made all the hardships worthwhile.

Ron had an Italian prisoner of war named Bruno as his assistant at the cinema. *Such an artistic soul, despite being a prisoner,* I thought as I watched him work. Bruno was really nice and talented at drawing portraits. One day, we sat among the rocks while Bruno drew a beautiful head and shoulders picture of me.

"Please, sit still just a moment longer, signora," Bruno would say, his pencil moving expertly across the paper. I still have that special drawing. But we got into trouble when someone saw us and reported Ron for fraternising with the prisoners.

"What were you thinking, Clark?" the commanding officer demanded. "Prisoners are not your friends!" *But Bruno seemed so harmless, so human,* I remember thinking as Ron endured the severe scolding.

The boarding house where we stayed was owned by people who loved throwing parties. One Saturday night, I had just finished cooking a roast lamb for dinner. *The aroma filled our tiny room,* I recalled proudly. The owners had friends over, their laughter drifting up from downstairs. The next morning, our delicious lamb was gone! "Well," Ron said with a resigned smile, "I suppose someone enjoyed a midnight feast." *I hope their guests appreciated all my hard work,* I thought ruefully.

After about 6 weeks, the Cowra camp closed down. I went back home to Adelaide while Ron was sent to Sydney for leave and his next posting.

"We'll be together again soon," he promised as we said goodbye.

He came home for a short break before returning to Sydney to work on the mobile cinema units for a few weeks. Then Ron was sent back to the Greta reinforcement battalion area. *Just when I thought we'd settled somewhere,* I thought anxiously. After some time there, he got orders to go to Rabaul in New Guinea as a projectionist at the Prisoner of War and Internee camp headquarters. He stayed in Rabaul for about a year.

While Ron was in Rabaul, his brother Laurie's story was unfolding. Before leaving England, Laurie had met a girl named Isobel and proposed to her.

"You'll never believe what Laurie's done!" Ron's mother told me excitedly, reading his letter.

Their ship had to return to port unexpectedly, so Laurie and Isobel decided to get married right then and there! We were all so excited, but sadly, Laurie had to leave his new bride behind to finish his duties. At least he put plans in motion for Isobel to join him back home soon.

While Ron was still away in 1946, Isobel arrived from England. I had been writing letters to her after Laurie returned home, hoping it would make her feel welcome. But when Isobel came, I hardly spoke to her because I didn't want to get in the way of her reconnecting with the rest of the family.

Years later, Isobel confided in me: "I was so hurt when you seemed distant," she said. "I had looked forward to having a sister in you."

If only I had known then what I know now, I thought regretfully. Even back then, it took me a long time to feel comfortable around new people. I wasn't an outgoing person at all.

Thinking back on my shyness with Isobel, I realise how much our early experiences shape us. That timid young woman who held back from welcoming a new sister-in-law would eventually find her voice and confidence, becoming the heart of our growing family. *Life has a way of teaching us exactly what we need to learn. I reflect now, even if the lessons take years to fully understand.*

After Isobel arrived in Australia, both Laurie and Ron had motorcycles. The four of us would often go out together, with Isobel and me riding on the backs of their bikes. "Hold on tight!" Ron would call over his shoulder as we zoomed down the roads. We did this even when we were pregnant with our first babies!

"Are you sure this is safe?" I remember asking Isobel once, both of us balancing our growing bellies.

We were so young and carefree then, I think now with a shake of my head. Looking back, it was incredibly risky, and we were so lucky nothing happened to cause a miscarriage. *Youth makes you feel invincible,* I realise now, *but God was watching over us and our precious cargo.*

In September 1947, Laurie and Isobel welcomed twins - a son named Tony and a daughter named Joy. "Double the blessing!" we all exclaimed. Now, 54 years later, Tony is married to Gail and they have two children of their own, plus a grandchild. Joy married Bob Northcott, and they have two daughters and one grandchild. *Who could have imagined, back then, how our family tree would branch and blossom?*

Years later, in 2001, when we visited Sydney for Anzac Day, we travelled by train from Sydney to Melbourne. As we passed through the station called "Harden," I grabbed Ron's hand.

"Look!" I exclaimed, "This is where I changed trains that night!"

The memories came rushing back like a flood - the lonely wait in the dark, the smell of the coal smoke, the nervous excitement of a young bride travelling to meet her husband.

That's where I had changed trains on my way to meet Ron in Cowra in 1946! Sitting on that modern train, with its comfortable seats and clean restrooms, I couldn't help but smile at how far we'd come. *What would that anxious young woman think,* I wondered, *if she could see me now, surrounded by the life we built?*

Looking back, I wouldn't have it any other way. An ever-growing family was one of my greatest dreams realised - a legacy of love to carry forth long after I'm gone. *Each new baby, each wedding, each milestone has been a blessing that I so cherish;* I reflect. Now, as I write these memories, I understand that our story was never just about Ron and me. It was about a generation learning to build lives amid uncertainty, about families expanding and adapting, about love that grows stronger through challenges.

"Remember when..." Ron and I often say to each other now, and though some details may have faded with time, the feelings remain as vivid as ever. Even if I can't recall every detail these days, the most important thing is the feelings those memories spark - of community, belonging, and being eternally woven together. *In the end,* I think to myself, *it's not the perfect memory that matters, but the perfect love that created it.*

CHAPTER 5

In the Warmth of Hope

My life's biggest dream was finally realised in the warmth of Teddy's tiny body snuggled against mine. *Is this real?* I wondered in awe. *After all the waiting, all the hoping, he's finally here.* How does it feel to hold your newborn baby for the very first time? What would that feel like after waiting and hoping for so long? The soft warmth of their tiny body, their sweet baby smell, those brand new eyes blinking up at you. For me, that magical moment finally happened when my son Teddy was born.

Across Australia, a generation of war brides like me was finally getting their chance at motherhood as our soldiers returned home. In the maternity wards, every bed was full, every nursery overflowing with new life. *We're all part of something bigger*, I thought as I looked down the row of beds at all the new mothers. We were all part of the great baby boom that would reshape our nation.

While Ron was away serving, I continued working during our first year of marriage. I got a job at the Myers dressmaking factory on King William Street, near South Terrace. Living alone in just one small room on Cheltenham Street in Malvern, my wages felt tiny. *Three more miles to go,* I'd tell myself on those long walks, my feet aching. Even with the allowance from Ron's Army pay, there were many times I couldn't afford the bus or tram fare. I'd have to walk the long three miles to the Unley Post Office just to collect my allowance money.

Those were tough times, with ration coupons needed for basics like clothes, butter, sugar, meat, and even petrol. "How many coupons for butter this week?" was our constant refrain. Travel was really restricted. But life was still better for us than for people suffering in England and Europe after the war. *We're lucky, all things considered,* I'd remind myself. We learned to make do with what little we had.

Six months into our marriage, after my trip to Cowra to reunite with Ron, I became pregnant with our first baby. *Finally!* I remember thinking with joy. It took longer than I'd hoped - I was so eager to have a child right away! The entire nine months were miserable. Any whiff of cooking food made me violently ill at any hour of the day or night. "It'll all be worth it," my mother would comfort me as I retched. *And she was right,* I think now. But feeling that constant nausea was worth it to have my dream of a baby finally come true.

For some of the pregnancy, I stayed with my sister Wilma and her husband Bill. Other times, I lived with my own Mum and Dad. My memory's foggy on the exact details now.

Finally, on Monday, June 24th, the labour pains began. "It's time," I whispered to myself, both terrified and thrilled. I was admitted to the hospital on Tuesday, the 25th and laboured all the way until Wednesday evening, June 26th, 1947. At around 8 pm, our son Ronald Edwin Jr. - "Teddy" for short - entered the world.

The doctor who delivered Teddy was Dr Glastonbury at Quambi Hospital on South Terrace. "Never mind the ashes," the nurses would say, rolling their eyes. An odd fellow, he was a compulsive chain smoker. At each monthly checkup, he just puffed away constantly, ashes hanging perilously from his cigarette the whole time. *How does he not set everything on fire?* I'd wonder. I'll never understand how he performed surgeries like that! But I didn't care about his smoking habits one bit. Cradling my long-awaited newborn son, all the morning sickness and discomforts instantly melted away.

Teddy was a beautiful baby, but his hair refused to curl no matter how hard I tried! "Stay down!" I'd plead as I wet his stubborn cowlick. We have an adorable photo of him in his high chair with his hair sticking straight up in the centre. It still does that to this day.

"There's a call from New Guinea for Mrs Clark," I heard the nurse say. Ron was informed of Teddy's arrival while stationed in New Guinea. Back then, new Mums weren't allowed out of bed for 10 days after giving birth. But Ron got his dates mixed up and called the hospital from New Guinea on the 9th day, hoping to speak to me.

"Rules are rules," the matron said firmly.

I was in the room right across the hall, but the strict matron wouldn't let me out of bed to answer the phone. *So close yet so far,* I thought tearfully. I felt so upset that Ron had to call back the next day instead. *Just one more day,* I consoled myself, *and I can finally share our joy with him.*

Everything went smoothly, and I looked forward to going home on the usual 14th day. But the hospitals were overflowing with post-war baby booms. *Like a grand reunion of war brides,* I thought, watching the bustling hallways. Quambi was packed, with patients waiting in the hallways.

"Mrs Clark," the matron asked, "do you have help at home? The doctor might release you early." *Home a day early!* My heart leapt at the thought. Of course, I was thrilled at the idea of going home to my Mum's place!

They tried contacting the doctor, and in the meantime, someone else was put in my bed. *Finally going home,* I thought excitedly, but then: "Absolutely not," came the doctor's firm response. The only bed left was in a private room, so that's where they moved me for one night. *So quiet,* I thought in the darkness. Too quiet. I just cried and cried, feeling so alone in that private room without any other Mums nearby to chat with.

Thankfully, I pulled myself together and we went home the next day as planned. What an exciting time it was, with Teddy being the first grandchild born on our side of the family. "Our little pioneer," Dad would say proudly. Ron's mother already had her two grandkids, Valmai and Billy.

For a couple of weeks, I stayed with my Mum and Ron to get used to caring for a newborn. *How strange, I thought, that they never let us practice in the hospital.* We didn't get any hands-on practice there at all. At feedings, we could only unwrap the babies' blankets to see them, never picking them up.

"For all we know," I whispered to another new mum, "they could be showing us the same baby over and over!"

After those first few weeks, Teddy and I moved in with Wilma and her husband Bill on Spencer Street in Cowandilla. We had just one room in their house, and I cooked and cleaned for us. *Everything has its place in Wilma's world,* I thought admiringly. Wilma was an incredibly neat housekeeper who stuck to a strict schedule - washing on Mondays, ironing Tuesdays, cleaning on Fridays, rain or shine. "No need to fuss," she'd say when I tried to help. I didn't have too much work to do around her spotless house.

We mainly stayed in the kitchen, where the warm wood stove was. On chilly nights, we'd open the oven door and stick our feet inside to stay toasty.

"This is the life," I'd sigh contentedly as Wilma and I would chat while Bill played beautiful tunes on the piano in the living room. *Such talent,* I marvelled. He was so talented, playing by ear without any sheet music.

I loved taking Teddy out in his pram to do our shopping.

But one day, in a total mum-brain moment, I accidentally left him parked outside the fruit and veg shop! *Where's the pram?* The panic hit me like a wave when I realised. The owner knew me and kept an eye on Teddy until I came running back, frantic.

"Don't worry," he chuckled, "happens to the best of mums." I was so grateful and learned my lesson about double-checking I had the baby before leaving any store!

One time, I left Teddy with Wilma to get my hair permed. *He'll love my new look,* I thought excitedly. When I returned, looking so different, the poor little guy didn't even recognise his own mother!

"Come to Mummy," I coaxed, but he fussed and cried, refusing to be consoled by me for quite a while. *Note to self,* I thought, *no more dramatic hair changes until he's older!*

Around 6 months old, just before Ron returned from his post in New Guinea, I made the long train trip to Melbourne to finally reunite with him after so many months apart. *Will he recognise me?* My heart raced with anticipation. When we arrived back in Adelaide, Wilma brought Teddy to the station so Ron could meet his son. "There he is!" I whispered to Ron, watching his eyes light up. The first word that came out of Teddy's mouth when he saw us was "Choo choo!" - so clever for a 6-month-old.

"Did he just...?" Ron asked in disbelief. *Our clever little man,* I thought proudly. Watching that new father/son bond sparking to life, my heart swelled with pure joy and gratitude. *This is how it should be - the three of us together at last.*

Teddy hit his baby milestones a bit slowly - getting his first teeth at 5 months, crawling around 10 months, and walking at 16 months. "He'll do things in his own time," Mum would reassure me. But he was such a laidback, happy guy, content to take his precious time.

After returning from his post in New Guinea, Ron came home on leave. He reported for duty at Keswick for a little while before being sent to the Torrens Training Depot.

"We're expecting Sergeant Clerk," they said, puzzled.

There was some confusion when he arrived - they were expecting a "Sergeant Clerk" but got Sergeant Clark instead!

Once that little mix-up got sorted out, Ron received new orders sending him to Ingleburn in New South Wales. *Here we go again,* I sighed inwardly. The reason? To properly train as a Sergeant Clerk. I can only imagine how Ron felt getting shuffled from base to base like that. He'd already been through so much travelling and getting relocated during the war years. Just when we thought we could settle into a routine at home, the Army moved him somewhere new. But Ron took it all in stride, as he always did.

"Orders are orders," he'd say with that calm smile of his. He was a steady sailor navigating whatever choppy waters life sent his way. I admired his ability to just go with the flow and make the best of every situation.

Finally, in late 1951, Ron received his longer-term posting at the Woodside camp in South Australia. *A real home at last,* I thought hopefully. For the next three years, until the end of 1954, that became our home base. During his time at Woodside, Ron oversaw seven different intakes of young National Service recruits.

Watching squad after squad of fresh-faced boys arrive must have felt surreal. *They're just children,* I'd catch Ron thinking sometimes. Not so long ago, he was in their boots - a bright-eyed teenager shipping off to fight, not knowing what horrors awaited. I'll never forget the weary look in Ron's eyes whenever a new group of soldiers-in-training arrived. In those unguarded moments, I caught glimpses of the wartime battles still raging in his memories.

"Ready to learn, sir!" they'd call out eagerly. The National Service lads' nervous excitement reminded him of his own youthful naivete about to be shattered. Yet Ron always snapped back to the present, clear-eyed and resolved to transform those raw recruits into battlefield-ready men.

"Listen carefully, men," he'd say, his voice carrying the weight of experience.

Next, he'd pour every ounce of hard-won knowledge into drilling them for the realities ahead. It couldn't have been easy reliving those personal traumas day after day. But there was a quiet nobility in the way Ron sublimated his pain into prepping the next wave of defenders. In his own way, he was preventing others from having their innocence ravaged like his was.

For all the emotional turmoil, Ron's steadfast leadership and training prowess paid off in 1952. That year, he received a promotion to Warrant Officer - an immense honour capping years of dedicated service. "Congratulations, Warrant Officer Clark," they said, but I could see in his eyes that home was calling louder than duty now. As the months and years marched on, I watched my stoic husband's military mask slip more frequently. Ron's face betrayed his longing to trade life on the road for staying put with his family.

He's ready, I thought one evening, watching him with Teddy. So, in 1954, after presiding over one final intake of National Service recruits, Ron decided it was time. He put in for his discharge from the Army that year. "Time to come home for good," he said simply. We were finally going to have a real chance at a stable, rooted life together as civilians.

I'll never forget the day Teddy's little sister was born. *Our family is growing,* I thought excitedly. Teddy was 2 years and 3 months old then. We were living with Auntie Viv, Uncle Jack, and their daughter Hazel in a Housing Trust home on 4th Avenue in Woodville Gardens. *Like sardines in a tin,* I'd think sometimes, but we made it work. Hazel was just one year younger than Teddy. The three kids played together a lot since the house felt a bit crowded with two families under one roof. But it wasn't too bad since Ron was still in the Army, and Uncle Jack served in the Air Force, so they weren't always home.

On Friday, September 16th, 1949, I went into labour. *Here we go again,* I thought, remembering Teddy's birth. Dr

Glastonbury, the same doctor who delivered Teddy, was there again at the little nursing home in Mile End.

After many long hours, a nurse finally bursted with a big smile, "You have a baby girl, and she was born with a caul!"

A caul? *What on earth is that?* I had no idea what that meant. I pictured my newborn daughter with some kind of strange growth or extra body part. Panic started creeping in as I wondered if something was wrong. "Is... is she alright?" I managed to ask.

But the nurse could see the concern on my face. "Don't worry," she reassured me, "A caul is good luck! It's just a piece of membrane covering the baby's face at birth."

Relief washed over me as she explained this bizarre phenomenon I'd never heard of before.

"Here," she said, carefully preserving the delicate tissue.

The nurse even kept that thin piece of stretchy skin for me since it was considered so lucky and rare. "This means your daughter will never drown," she said matter-of-factly. "Sailors used to pay lots of money to have one of these cauls for protection at sea."

My lucky little girl, I thought, gazing at my daughter. I couldn't believe this little miracle had happened to my Raelene Carol on the very day she came into the world. Staring at that wrinkly piece of birth tissue, I knew it would become a cherished family keepsake representing hope and safekeeping through life's stormiest waters.

Over the years, our family kept growing like a garden in full bloom. "Another blessing," we'd say with each new addition. Auntie Viv and Uncle Jack adopted a daughter named Jacqueline, though she goes by Jacqui now. A few years later, they had a son, too, named Darryl. Jacqui lives in England these days. She's married to John Hackney, and they have two kids of their own - James and Louisa.

After Viv and Jack divorced, Viv moved the whole family to Melbourne for work. That's where she met and married her second husband, Brian Auld. Before long, our little Woodville Gardens house felt bursting at the seams. *We can barely turn around in here,* I thought, watching the children play. With Teddy, Raelene, Hazel, Jacqui, and Darryl all underfoot, the walls seemed to close in tighter each day. "We need our own space," Ron said one evening, and I couldn't agree more.

We applied for a Housing Trust loan and built a beautiful three-bedroom house on English Avenue in Clovelly Park. "Can you believe the price?" we'd marvel. Can you imagine - the whole double brick place only cost 1,100 pounds, or about $2,500 back then! The land alone was 75 pounds, or $150. *Our very own piece of paradise,* I thought proudly. Nowadays, that same house would easily go for $120,000 or $140,000. My, how times have changed!

So many incredible memories were made in that Clovelly Park home over the years. Yet, there are strange gaps in my memory, too. *How curious the mind can be,* I reflect now. I'll never forget Teddy's little sister Raelene arriving with her miraculous caul. But for the life of me, I can't recall much about when Bryce, our third child, was born later on in that very same house! *Memory plays such tricks on us,* I think with a touch of sadness. How could I possibly forget something so enormously life-changing?

The pregnancy felt like a blur until the day Bryce was born. *Just breathe,* I kept telling myself. I'll never forget April 20th, 1951, at the Queen Victoria Maternity Hospital in Rose Park. As the contractions grew stronger, I could feel beads of sweat forming on my forehead. "You're doing wonderfully," the nurse encouraged. The pain was intense, but I tried to breathe slowly like the nurses instructed. Finally, after what felt like an eternity, I heard Bryce's first cries fill the room. *That beautiful sound,* I thought through tears of joy. Holding my newborn son, all the aches melted away.

Not long after, Ron got orders to move to Woodside. "We'll make it work," Ron assured me, but my heart was heavy. We decided to live on the army base at Inverbrackie since it was cheaper and closer to Ron's work. Selling our house on English Avenue was tough - it held so many memories. *Our first real home,* I thought sadly. Our temporary flat in Balhannah felt cramped right away. Then we moved into a caravan in someone's field in Woodside while waiting for our quarters.

I'll never forget 8-month-old Bryce's sad eyes as the rain poured endlessly outside our tiny metal home. *Tap tap tap* went the raindrops, like nature mocking our discomfort.

The soggy ground prevented him from playing, and he grew frustrated being cooped up. "Soon, darling," I'd whisper, trying to comfort him. Seeing my cheerful baby's spirit dimmed by the gloomy caravan broke my heart. I longed for us to finally settle somewhere bright and comfortable.

Living in the cramped caravan with Teddy, Raelene, and little Bryce felt like we were stuffed into a tiny metal can. But finally, the day came when our family could move into the new house at Inverbrackie. *This should be perfect,* I thought hopefully. I should have been overjoyed, but something didn't feel right. As we unpacked boxes and arranged the furniture, a sickly smell hung in the air. *Oh no,* I thought as nausea swept over me. The fresh paint and new flooring made my stomach churn. Before I knew it, I couldn't stop vomiting. The awful smells triggered my morning sickness, even though I was already pregnant again.

After a few miserable days, the doctor admitted me to the Woodside Hospital. "You need rest," he insisted. I felt so helpless lying in that bed, too ill to even cook for my three young kids back home. *My poor babies,* I worried. Poor Teddy, Raelene, and Bryce were surviving on just Weetbix morning, noon, and night. I wondered if the bland cereal would turn them off to it forever.

One afternoon, a nurse brought my tray of food. When she returned to the kitchen, I overheard her say, "I think that new patient is dying." *Am I really that bad?* My heart sank. I wanted this pregnancy so badly, but how could I care for a newborn if I couldn't even keep down a cracker?

The kind hospital cook, Jean Dewhirst, became a dear friend to our family. "Don't you worry about a thing," she'd say with her warm smile. Whenever I had to go back for my pregnancies, she and her husband, Tom, offered to help look after Ron and the kids. Jean's support meant the world to me during those difficult times.

After nine long months of morning sickness, it was finally time to give birth again. I was admitted to the Woodside Hospital, with Dr Jungfer overseeing everything. "He may be gruff," the nurses would say, "but he knows what he's doing." Some people thought he had a gruff bedside manner, but I was just grateful to have an experienced doctor I could trust.

For two weeks after the delivery, I rested in the hospital. *I hope everything's alright at home,* I fretted. I wondered how Ron and the others were managing at home with Jean's help. She was a wonderful cook, but housekeeping wasn't her strongest suit. When Jean arrived to pick me up, I could tell something was amiss the moment we walked through the back door. *Oh my,* I thought, taking in the scene. The floor was soaked, with clothes strewn everywhere. Jean had overfilled the copper tub for washing, and it had overflowed. The whole room looked like a swimming pool!

Part of me wanted to turn around and go back to my sanitised hospital room. *But look how hard she tried,* I reminded myself. But Jean had worked so hard taking care of everyone. I couldn't let a bit of household chaos ruin her efforts. "You've been absolutely wonderful," I told her sincerely. Stepping gingerly through the puddles, I gave Jean a hug. She beamed with pride as I held our beautiful newborn daughter for the first time. "Welcome home, little one," I whispered. We named her Lesley Ann.

Living among the officers and other residents on the Inverbrackie base was a fascinating experience. *Each window holds a different story,* I'd think during my evening walks. Our neighbours came from such diverse walks of life, united by their military service. "Morning, Mrs Clark!" they'd call out as children played together in shared yards. No matter our ranks, we were all living and raising our families together in this shared community. *Like a village within a village,* I mused. I wondered what kinds of stories and perspectives each household held behind its doors.

Just when I thought our struggles were over, a new storm rolled in. *That familiar feeling of uncertainty,* I thought, as I cradled baby Lesley Ann close. A chill ran down my spine. The dark clouds gathering outside echoed the uneasy feeling in my heart. "We've weathered worse," I whispered to my sleeping infant. What fresh challenges awaited us? I took a deep breath, preparing for whatever lay ahead. *We're stronger than we know,* I reminded myself. Our family's resilience would be tested once more.

Years now, I realise that my journey into motherhood was shaped as much by the rhythms of post-war Australia as by my own maternal instincts. *We were all finding our way together,* I reflect. We were part of a generation rebuilding not just families, but a nation. The challenges we faced - the rationing, the constant moves, the separations - taught us resilience. *Every sacrifice was building something greater,* I understand now. But they also taught us the importance of community, of helping hands and shared understanding.

In raising our children during those transformative years, we weren't just nurturing the next generation - we were helping to birth a new Australia, one baby at a time. *Our children would inherit the peace we fought so hard to win,* I think with pride. Each diaper changed, each meal cooked, each bedtime story read was a small act of hope for the future we dreamed of building.

CHAPTER 6

The Journey into the Unknown

The earth moved beneath us that night in 1954. Not metaphorically – literally shook our world apart and back together again.

What do you do when your whole world starts trembling? When the very ground beneath your feet betrays you? These thoughts raced through my mind as I jolted awake to what sounded like a massive truck barreling through the field behind our house at Inverbrackie Army Base.

"Ron!" I whispered urgently, shaking my husband's shoulder. "Ron, wake up!"

Before he could respond, our bed slid six inches across

the floor with an awful screech. The whole building began to shake violently.

"The children!" The thought hit me like lightning. My heart pounding against my ribs, I leapt from the bed. "Kids, get up! Something's happening!" The children's faces were pale in the darkness as I pulled them from their beds.

"Mum, what's happening?" Ted's voice quavered, his small hand clutching mine.

"Just stay close to me, love," I managed, trying to keep my voice steady. "We need to get outside."

We burst through the front door to find the entire neighbourhood already huddled in their pyjamas on the street. Mrs Thompson from next door stood clutching her dressing gown, her hair in curlers.

"It's an earthquake!" someone shouted. I can't remember who, but the voice seems to ring in my mind even years after.

I pulled my babies close, silently praying the violent quaking would stop before the houses caved in on us. *Please, God, keep us safe. Keep all of us safe.*

When the terrifying rumbling finally ceased, neighbours started cautiously inspecting their homes for damage. That's what life at Inverbrackie was like – a community bound together by circumstances both ordinary and extraordinary. One minute you're sleeping peacefully, the next you're standing in your nightclothes with your neighbours, all pretence of military hierarchy forgotten.

"Everyone alright, Martha?" Ron asked Mrs Thompson, his

sergeant's authority naturally emerging even in a crisis.

"Yes, thank heaven," she replied, still shaking. "Though I doubt I'll sleep another wink tonight."

"Put the kettle on," I found myself saying. "Everyone's welcome at ours for a cuppa."

That's how we ended up hosting an impromptu midnight tea party, all of us still in our nightclothes, children dozing on the floor while adults murmured about fault lines and tremors. It was moments like these that showed the true nature of our community.

Life at Inverbrackie was complex, a delicate twist of rank and relationships. The social hierarchy was clear as polished brass: officers and their families occupied one sphere, other ranks another. With Ron being a sergeant and later a warrant officer, we straddled both worlds.

"The officers' wives can be right proper snobs," I overheard one woman complain at the base shop one morning.

"Hush now," her friend whispered, glancing around nervously. "You never know who might be listening."

I pretended to be absorbed in selecting vegetables, but her words stuck with me. We tried to stay neutral, walking that careful line between worlds. Ron's position meant we got along with both groups, but it also meant we saw the tensions that simmered beneath the surface.

The base itself was a collection of simple houses and buildings, but it was the people who gave it life. Every morning, the clip-clop of hooves announced Ted Downs's horse-drawn cart delivering fresh bread. His wife Shirley would often stop for a chat, their five children – four girls and one boy named Carol, of all things – tumbling around her like puppies.

"You wouldn't believe what Carol did yesterday," Shirley would laugh, leaning on our fence. "Caught him trying to teach the youngest to ride the bread horse!"

Those lighter moments balanced the darker ones that inevitably came with living in such close quarters.

One night, the sound of pounding on our door jolted us from sleep.

"Please, help me!" Our neighbour stood there, tears streaming down her face, a bruise darkening on her cheek. Her husband, a mountain of a man, had struck her.

I pulled her inside while Ron stood in the doorway, his jaw tight. We both knew he couldn't intervene physically – the man was twice his size. Sometimes courage meant knowing when to step back and find another way to help.

"Stay here tonight," I whispered, leading her to our spare room. "We'll sort things out in the morning."

Then there was the morning that stopped all our hearts. I was hanging washing when I noticed the unusual silence from the house across the street. Doors locked, blinds drawn at 10 AM. Strange for a home with young children.

The news spread through the base in whispers: their three-year-old son had accidentally fallen on their eighteen-month-old daughter overnight. The baby didn't survive.

How do you comfort parents who've lost a child? I wondered, standing at my window, watching the father's military colleagues awkwardly bringing casseroles and condolences. Rank and reputation meant nothing in the face of such tragedy. We were just parents, holding our children closer, sharing in the universal fear of loss.

But there were joyful times too. The cocktail parties at the sergeants' mess sparkled with laughter and dance. I remember one particular evening, getting ready while Ron adjusted his uniform for the hundredth time.

"You look handsome enough to be an officer," I teased, smoothing his collar.

"Don't let the other sergeants hear you say that," he winked back.

Military parades brought pageantry to our days. The children would stand transfixed as the bands marched past, Ron straight-backed and proud in formation. I'd catch myself swelling with pride, watching him lead his men.

New experiences enriched our lives in unexpected ways. The walnut tree beside the bakery introduced me to flavours I'd never known growing up in the city.

Yet beneath the orderly surface of military life ran currents of drama that could explode at any moment. Like the night a woman's screams pierced the evening calm.

"He's got an axe!" The cry went up.

We watched in horror as her husband stood at their front door, the axe glinting in the porch light. The sound of splintering wood echoed through our tidy streets as he swung it through the door. The memory of that sound still makes me shudder.

Bang! Bang! Bang!

Three solid hits before the MPs arrived. In moments like these, the facade of military discipline crumbled, revealing the messy humanity beneath.

Living that close together, we were all in each other's business whether we liked it or not. We were united in our vulnerability as imperfect people muddling through the beauty and heartbreak of life together. That's what made Inverbrackie special - not the military hierarchy or the social politics, but the way we came together when it really mattered.

Those early days shaped me in ways I never expected. Each crisis and celebration, each moment of community support and shared grief, helped transform me from that doe-eyed military wife into someone stronger. I would need that strength for the challenges ahead - Ron's decision to leave the Army, our move to the farm, and the deepest heartache a mother could face.

But first, I had to master those treacherous mountain roads. Learning to drive those challenging rural roads was more than just gaining a new skill - it was my rite of passage into independence. At first, I dreaded Ron's attempts to make me practice during our inbound city trips while he rode shotgun.

"You've got to learn sometime," he'd say firmly, ignoring my white-knuckled grip on the steering wheel. "What if there's an emergency with the kids?"

"He's right", I'd think, but that knowledge didn't make the blind curves and steep grades any less terrifying with my family's lives in my inexperienced hands.

Our humble mode of transport added an extra level of adventure: a Morris Cowley with a canvas top and plastic side windows instead of glass. Upon reflection, I can't believe we felt so safe cocooned in what was basically a covered wagon! I'll never forget the rattle and flap of those thin barriers as the winds buffeted us up and down each mountain pass.

Taking leisurely Sunday drives through the lush, winding hills to visit Viv, my Mum and Dad in the city made for picturesque family days - when the weather cooperated. I'd often marvel at how my sister Viv maneuvered her tiny Ford Anglia over those steep mountain passes! The usually 90-minute trip probably took her double that in such an underpowered car. But we never worried about safety - that's just how different things were in those innocent times.

Woodside seemed to always be freezing cold and drenched in rain. After visiting Nana Hulbert or Nana Clark in the city, we'd often drive home through a thick, soupy fog. The headlights could barely slice through the dense greyness enveloping the road ahead.

"Roll down the windows," I'd instruct the children, "or the car will fog up inside."

"But Mum, it's freezing!" they'd protest, huddling together under blankets - even the dog joined their warmth-seeking pile.

"Better cold than blind," I'd reply, though the icy air bit at our exposed faces as I squinted, straining to make out the road's edges.

More than once, I lost sight of where we were going and accidentally veered off the pavement. How we safely made those treacherous trips back, I'll never know. I suppose the lack of other traffic helped a bit. Still, nighttime drives through those blind country fogs were some of the most white-knuckled journeys of my life.

One particularly harrowing drive home sticks out in my memory like a photograph frozen in time. I was behind the wheel with all four kids and the dog crammed inside. As we crossed the bridge into Murray Bridge, I gave the steering wheel a hard crank to make the turn towards Parrakie. But the car didn't respond - it just ploughed straight ahead off the road!

"Mum, watch out!" the kids screamed as we hurtled towards what looked like a sheer cliff face in the fog.

"Dear God, please don't let this be how it ends", I prayed silently, pumping the brakes frantically. But the steering wheel went horrifyingly loose in my hands. There was no regaining control.

Just when I braced for impact, the cliff turned out to be a shallow embankment. We slammed into the muddy slope with a bone-jarring thud, finally skidding to a stop. My heart pounded out of my chest, but miraculously, we were all unhurt.

"Is everyone alright?" I called out, twisting around to check on my precious cargo. A chorus of shaken but positive responses helped my racing heart begin to slow.

A mechanic from a nearby gas station raced over to inspect the damage. "It's your tie rod," he announced after a quick look.

"Snapped clean through - that's why you lost all steering control."

As he explained how the broken part had left us completely unable to steer or brake properly, my knees went weak. If that flimsy cliff hadn't stopped our momentum, we could have careened into a steep ditch or ravine and met a far grimmer fate.

"Someone up there must be watching over you folks," the mechanic remarked, helping arrange for a tow.

Bruised but thankful to be alive, we somehow made it home that night. Shaken, I gave thanks for the unexpected obstacle that abruptly halted our skid towards disaster - and silently prayed we'd never again have such a brush with tragedy on those haunting, fog-shrouded country roads.

When Ron finally declared me ready to venture into town alone, a huge weight lifted from my shoulders. Yes, the kids were still in the backseat, but at least I didn't have to worry about impressing Ron anymore! Each solo trip built my confidence, even when Mother Nature seemed determined to test my newfound skills.

Those early days of white-knuckle solo drives, juggling errands with childcare, and navigating treacherous weather conditions hardened my resolve. Every successful journey home made me a little braver, a little more self-reliant. Little did I know how much I would need that courage in the years ahead, as our family faced changes that would take us far from these familiar mountain roads to an entirely different kind of challenge...

❄

That winter of 1954, Ron came home with news that made my heart skip a beat. "I've been thinking," he said, settling into his chair. "I want to try my hand at farming."

I nearly dropped the pot I was holding. "Farming?" I echoed, trying to keep my voice steady. "But Ron, we don't know the first thing about running a farm."

"I was born on a farm," he replied with that determined look I knew so well. "That ought to count for something."

Oh, how naive we were, us greenhorn city folk. If only we'd known what we were walking into.

Ron put his name in at the Employment Office, where farmer Len Gersch discovered him. I remember standing in our kitchen when Ron came home from the interview, his eyes bright with excitement. "We've got a place," he announced. "Three bedrooms on the Gersch property at Sandilands, York Peninsula. The kids will have other children to play with - Len's boys Malcolm and Robert are around Ted's age."

"What about the work?" I asked, already worrying about the change ahead.

"Hard work never killed anyone," Ron said with a confidence I wished I could share.

The reality hit us like a sledgehammer. Len ran that farm like a military operation, but harder - if that was even possible. I'd watch Ron go out before dawn, and he wouldn't return until well past dark. Sometimes I'd stand at the window as the sun set, thinking, "How can anyone work such long hours and still stand upright?"

Every night around 8 pm, Ron would finally stagger home, barely able to keep his eyes open long enough to kiss the children goodnight. Even Sundays brought no rest at first. While the Gersch family attended Lutheran church services, Ron and the other hands still toiled through the day. "This isn't living", I thought to myself. "This is surviving. "

It wasn't until we started attending church with the Gersches that we got any semblance of a weekend. "The Lord's day is for rest," Len had finally conceded, though I caught him eyeing the fields more than once during service.

Life had shifted from the familiar rhythms of oil-stained military bases to the nonstop, gruelling labour of a commercial farm. Everyone had to pitch in - even the children. "Ted, Bryce, time to gather the eggs!" I'd call out each morning. "And mind that ornery bull!"

Speaking of that ill-tempered beast, I'll never forget the day I glanced out to the yard and spotted little Raelene playing peacefully in the sandbox - with the massive bull just yards away, lazily munching grass! My heart stopped dead. "Dear God, don't let him move", I prayed silently, inching my way outside.

"Raelene, sweetheart," I whispered, trying to keep my voice calm, "stay very still for Mummy." I tiptoed closer, my heart thundering so loud I was sure the bull would hear it. When I finally scooped her up and made it back inside, my legs nearly gave out from relief.

My own days became an endless cycle of new tasks. "You'll

need to learn to milk the cows," Len's wife had told me matter-of-factly. "Morning and night, no exceptions."

The separator was my daily nemesis - a clunky contraption that needed every piece scrubbed spotless after each use. "You missed a spot," Len would say, inspecting it with military precision. "If it's not clean, the cream'll spoil."

Poor Ron struggled with his own battles. One evening, he came in looking particularly proud. "Built the biggest haystack you've ever seen," he announced over dinner. The next morning, I found him staring out the window, shoulders slumped. The entire stack had collapsed overnight.

"It's all about the angle," Len explained later, not unkindly. "Stack it too steep and gravity does the rest."

Then there was the sheep slaughtering. I'll never forget Ron's face the first time - pale and drawn as he tried to master the quick, clean stroke Len had demonstrated. The animal's suffering haunted us both that night. "I can't do it like Len can," Ron whispered in the dark. "Maybe I'm not cut out for this life."

"You're learning," I assured him, though my own doubts gnawed at me. "We all are."

The harvest season brought new challenges. Every night, Ron would come home with hands raw from stitching countless burlap sacks. I'd help him apply the beeswax and vinegar salve, neither of us mentioning the trembling in his fingers.

"How do you stand it?" I asked one evening as I bandaged yet another split fingertip.

"Same way we got through basic training," he replied with a weak smile. "One day at a time."

One day at a time became our mantra as we adjusted to this new life. Some nights, lying awake listening to the unfamiliar sounds of the farm - the low mooing of cows, the rustle of wind through the fields - I'd wonder if we'd made a terrible mistake. But then morning would come, bringing with it the sight of our children running freely through the open fields, their laughter mixing with the chorus of farm life, and I'd think maybe, just maybe, we could make this work.

Amidst all the endless toil of farm life, our family continued growing. On May 10th, 1955, our fifth child - a son we named Richard Kendrew, nicknamed Ricky - was born into our hectic brood. He seemed like such an easygoing baby at first, sleeping through most days and nights.

"What a blessing", I thought to myself as I watched him sleep peacefully in his cot. "Finally, a child who lets his mama catch her breath". I savoured those peaceful respites while juggling keeping the house and minding the rambunctious older four.

The morning of August 28th started routinely enough. "Ted, don't forget your lunch pail! Rae, please help Lesley with her shoes!" I called out, hurriedly prepping the children to catch the school bus. Ricky's cries rang out, but his fussing soon calmed. "He'll be fine until his usual feeding", I reassured myself, continuing with my chores. Ron had already left for another gruelling day's work on the farm.

When I finally went to get Ricky for his feeding, I'll never forget the spine-tingling horror of finding his tiny body frighteningly still and silent. My baby's lips were bluish, his skin cool to the touch.

"No, no, no, please God, no!" I shook him desperately, pleading for any sign of life. "Ricky, darling, wake up for Mama!" But it was too late. In that harrowing moment, my world collapsed.

Cradling Ricky's limp form, I raced outside. "Vera! Vera, help me, please!" My screams echoed across the yard. She came running, her face draining of colour when she saw what I held.

"I'll ring the doctor right away," she said, her voice trembling. "Then I'll fetch Ron from the fields."

The authorities had to be called since Ricky died at home. Those grim-faced police interrogated me endlessly. "You seem remarkably composed, Mrs Gersch," one officer said coldly, his eyes narrowing with suspicion.

"If only you could see the tempest raging inside me", I thought bitterly. Thank God Ron fiercely vouched for me. "My wife keeps her emotions private," he told them firmly. "She'll grieve in her own way, in her own time."

The doctors labelled it a "cot death" back then. Today it's called SIDS - Sudden Infant Death Syndrome. But no clinical term could convey the visceral, existential dread of awakening one morning to find your baby's spark of life inscrutably extinguished. As I stroked Ricky's miniature features, searing myself with every last detail, my mind screamed with questions no faith or science could ever answer. "What did I miss? Why didn't I check on him sooner? How could God let this happen to an innocent baby?"

When the doctor finally arrived, her three little Pekinese dogs yapping away in her car, I watched in numb disbelief as she wrapped Ricky's lifeless body in a scratchy hessian sack. "Like he's nothing but a parcel", my heart cried out. "My precious boy deserves better than this. "

After the doctor departed, Ron and I stood motionless in the backyard, twin pillars of stunned grief. The warm summer breeze carried birdsong and the faraway laughter of neighbourhood children.

"How can the world just go on like nothing's happened?" I whispered to Ron. He pulled me closer, unable to answer.

Then came the magpie's vicious swoop, pecking Ron's scalp. "Bloody hell!" he cursed, more from surprise than pain. I barely contained a primal scream. "Get away, you wretched bird!" I shouted, swatting at the air while examining Ron's bloodied crown. In all the years of our marriage, I'd never heard such language from him. *But today of all days, I thought, who could blame him?*

We stood there, man and wife united in tragedy, exposed, vulnerable, powerless against the senseless violence of ill-timed swoops and infant deaths alike. *Even nature mocks our grief,* I thought bitterly, watching the first droplets of Ron's blood speckle the dusty ground. They mirrored the crimson grief leaking from the ruptures in our shattered hearts.

Just when we thought we'd weathered the worst, tragedy struck again at our new home in Sandilands. Lesley fell deathly ill with whooping cough. I tortured myself with guilt, knowing I'd fallen behind on her vaccinations during our move.

I'll never forget hearing Lesley's tiny body racked by those horrific, violent coughing fits, leaving her gasping and vomiting until she became alarming thin and weak. That incessant, torturous barking sound still echoes in my nightmares. It took months for her to slowly regain her health and sunny energy.

What's the cruellest sight a parent can witness? For me, it was watching my sunny little Lesley wasting away, her tiny body racked by those violent, torturous coughing fits of whooping cough. I was terrified I would lose another child.

Hoping a family vacation could lift our spirits, the Dutschke relatives who attended the Gersch's church loaned us their caravan for a trip to Port Vincent. For a blessed few days, we basked in salty ocean air, building sandcastles and collecting shells along the peninsula's shores. Lesley's whooping cough finally seemed to ease as her cheeks regained their rosy glow.

Thank you, Lord, I prayed silently, noticing her cheeks finally regaining their rosy glow.

Life continued its relentless march forward. We moved to Dillowie, near Jamestown, and welcomed another girl, Glenda Jean, in the midst of back-breaking ranch work and fire scares that summer. On September 26th, 1956, the night I went into labour, our youngest child, Glenda Jean, was born at the Jamestown hospital.

We'd grown fond of the name Glenda from Don Gare's sister. And Jean honoured our dear friend Jean Dewhurst back in Woodside, who meant so much to us.

That night, the sky opened up in a ferocious storm - thunderous downpours, hail pelting the windows, and roads turning to muddy streams. But Ron bravely drove me to the hospital through it all. He wasn't about to let a little turbulent weather stop our baby girl's arrival into the world! Glenda Jean was born safe and sound the next morning.

"What a relief!" I exclaimed to the nurse. "No more being confined to those scratchy sheets for 10 long days!"

I still had to remain at the hospital for about two weeks total, but at least I could move around while little Glenda settled into our world. Her birth proved quite the adventure - she decided to arrive bottom first, with both tiny feet tucked up under her chin!

"A breech birth," Dr Bentley announced, studying my calm face with amazement. "Usually means a very difficult, complicated delivery. But you're handling it like a champion, Mrs Clark."

Her birth emerged as quite the adventure,too - she decided to arrive bottom first, with both tiny feet tucked up under her chin! But our respite was shattered when Glenda spiked a raging fever. She became dizzyingly ill, unable to stand without toppling over inside the cramped camper.

"We need to get her to a doctor," I urged Ron, terror gripping my heart. "Something's terribly wrong."

We rushed her to the nearest doctor in Curramulka, praying it was just a passing bug. The grim physician's words sent ice through my veins.

"Mrs Gersch, your daughter is showing signs of either golden staph, strep pneumonia, or meningitis," he said gravely. "I suspect meningitis. You need to get her to the Children's Hospital in North Adelaide immediately. She might not survive the night if we try treating her here."

"A mosquito bite?" I whispered in disbelief when he mentioned the possible cause. "Something so small could be so deadly?"

We had to scatter our other children to safety - Raelene staying with the kind Dutschkes who'd loaned us the caravan, Ted and Bryce to the Gersch farm, even though the owners weren't home. Lesley and I accompanied Glenda's lifeless body to the city hospital, her fate and our family's hanging in limbo's cruellest balance.

Was this another unthinkable tragedy unfolding? The thought tortured me as the city lights grew closer. I felt torn between clinging to hope and bracing for the unimaginable. *We've already lost one child,* I prayed silently, cradling Glenda's burning body. *Please don't let us lose another.*

As he advised us to go, I felt our mirage of a carefree family vacation shatter before my eyes. We whisked Glenda to the hospital while I scattered the other children to various friends and relatives.

Raelene stayed with the Dutschkes, who loaned the caravan, while Ted and Bryce went to the Gersch farm, even though the owners weren't home at the time.

Lesley and I accompanied Glenda's lifeless body to the city hospital, her fate and our family's hanging in limbo's cruellest balance.

Was this another unthinkable tragedy unfolding? As the city lights grew closer, I felt like I was torn between clinging to hope and bracing for the unimaginable. Glenda's life danced on a knife's edge, and my heart pounded, dreading what lay ahead.

CHAPTER 7

The Mystery of Glenda's Recovery

Mosquitoes, something so infinitesimally small, could carry death on their fragile wings. In the unforgiving landscape of rural Australia, where survival balanced on razor-thin margins, we learned that life's most brutal lessons often arrived in the most unexpected packages.

The night Glenda's life hung in precarious balance wasn't just another medical emergency. It was a crucible that would test everything we believed about family and hope. Her burning body, limp against my chest, whispered a stark truth: in this harsh world, love was our only shield against unthinkable loss.

As we drove to the hospital, Glenda's tiny body burned with

fever. The old Nash bounced along the dark roads, each bump a reminder of our fragile hopes. Len Gersch sold the old Nash to us, and I don't think it had ever been driven so fast before. As we sped towards the city lights, my heart pounded with dread. Each moment felt like an eternity.

At the hospital, the doctors confirmed Glenda had influenza meningitis and would need to stay for at least a week. Up until then, we had private medical coverage that we paid monthly premiums for. But a couple of months earlier, when money was tight, we hadn't paid the premiums, so now we were on the hook for whatever massive bill the hospital charged. In the end, Glenda ended up there for a whole month, not just a week.

The total cost came to around 400 pounds, which was $800 back then! The doctors struggled to find a cure until finally they had to open her skull on both sides of the front to check if anything was pressing on her brain, because she kept shaking so badly. Thankfully, they didn't find anything wrong. But when they stitched her back up, they had to insert two metal clips to cover the holes in her skull.

To this day, Glenda and I have letters from the hospital saying those clips must never be removed. I've always wondered if, when she was shaking so violently, maybe she had something like Parkinson's disease. And when they opened her skull, perhaps that released some pressure on her brain and cured whatever was causing the shakes. It's just a guess, but I did see a TV story once about relieving pressure on the brain to treat Parkinson's. Who knows? I'm sure even the doctors don't always have all the answers.

After Glenda finally left the hospital, we went back to the Gersch farm to pick up Ted and Bryce, and to the Dutschke family to get Raelene, who had been staying with them during that terrifying ordeal.

After a couple of years living and working on the Gersch farm in Sandilands, our family then moved to "Dillowie" - a big sheep property outside the town of Jamestown. Dillowie and a few other properties were owned by the Gare family.

The one we worked on was run by one of the sons, named Don, along with his wife Lois and their kids Dianne, Heather, Clive and Susan. The two youngest, Clive and Susan, were actually born while we lived there.

Rural life was a playground of danger and discovery. The kids had a blast learning to ride those horses they missed out on before. At the Dillowie sheep station, they could ride all they wanted - a freedom they never had on Len Gersch's farm. Back at Sandilands, Len Gersch didn't allow any horses on his farm because he thought they just cost money instead of making any. But here at the sheep station, the kids could ride all they wanted.

The work was pretty similar to Sandilands - still lots of early morning starts before the sun came up, and not getting home until late at night.

That meant our kids had to wake up extremely early to catch the school bus, and didn't return until well after dark. Long days for such young ones.

One new job we took on was collecting what they called "dead wool" off sheep that had died out in the paddocks.

It was an incredibly smelly, disgusting task, but we didn't mind because wool was fetching a very high price at that time. The stench would cling to our clothes until we could finally shower it off.

Not the most glamorous work, but those "dead wool" paychecks made it worthwhile!

So, while the labour was just as gruelling as farm life, living at Dillowie opened new experiences for the family too.

The kids had a blast learning to ride those horses they missed out on before. And even an unpleasant job like dead wool collecting couldn't dampen our spirits when it meant extra income for us all.

Ron had gotten pretty decent at riding horses by then, which was a good thing since his job often required rounding up and herding the sheep while on horseback.

One day, his horse came galloping back to the homestead without him! My heart raced, wondering if he'd been thrown or injured out in those vast paddocks alone.

Luckily, Ron strolled in a little while later, looking no worse for wear.

I don't remember exactly what spooked his horse - maybe a slithering snake on the trail? But he played it off like just another rugged day's work on the ranch.

Fire remained our biggest worry living out in that dry, rural area. During summer's hottest months, the men were frequently called away to help fight blazes that had sparked on neighbouring properties. The tiniest stray ember could rapidly exhaust their defences against those ferocious bushfires.

Good heavens, what's that noise? One sweltering afternoon, while Raelene and Lesley tried cooling off in the bathtub, we heard crackling outside and smelled smoke.

"Bryce!" I muttered under my breath, *"What have you done now?"*

Bryce had been messing about with matches, accidentally igniting the grass! Thankfully, the strong north wind was blowing away from the house that day.

"Quick, girls, get dressed!" I called out, grabbing a couple of old hessian bags. *"No time to waste,"* I thought, soaking them in the bathwater and racing outside.

The girls hurriedly dressed while the workers from the big house rushed over.

"We'll help beat back the flames!" one of the workers shouted.

As we secured the cleared perimeter with those wet bags, we managed to contain the blaze before it grew out of control.

While we settled in as a new family of seven at Dillowie, the older kids had their usual routines to keep up. Each morning, they'd hop on their bikes and pedal two kilometres down the long driveway to the main road. There, they'd catch the school bus heading for class at Whyte Yarcowie Area School. Their sole teacher, Mr Gordon Pearce, had his hands full instructing all seven grades together in that cramped one-room schoolhouse!

One afternoon, when the kids bounded off the bus, Bryce was nowhere to be found. The others innocently mentioned he'd been "catching a snake" before they left for home. Sure enough, we found Bryce at the trailhead, grinning and clutching a bottle with a living, venomous brown snake trapped inside!

"What on earth were you thinking?" I demanded, my voice trembling.

Bryce just grinned. "For show and tell, Mum! Mr Pearce will be so impressed!"

Impressed? More like terrified!

Thankfully, the smart teacher knew to douse the viper with methylated spirits right away, putting a permanent end to that risky exhibit. While I scolded Bryce for his dangerous antic, I couldn't help chuckling at the image of Mr Pearce's face when our son whipped out that bottled serpent!

At Dillowie, the kids all loved riding horses, which always made me fret in a whole different way. I remember Ted and Bryce decided to race their mounts through the homestead gates one day. In his haste, Ted misjudged the turn too sharply and went tumbling off, slamming face-first into a post! He staggered inside with his cheek gashed open and bleeding.

As I cleaned and bandaged that gruesome facial injury, I watched Ted's tough-kid bravado slowly crumble into frightened tears.

But just like Dr Bentley promised after Glenda's birth, little ones truly are resilient forces. Ted was right back in the saddle almost before his wound scabbed over, charging ahead into his next prank or misadventure.

Like the time he took a tumble into a thick patch of star thistles - we had to spend ages meticulously extracting those barbed needles from his tender legs and bottom. Ted cried and writhed with each pluck, but I knew deep down, he welcomed those prickly souvenirs as hard-earned badges of childhood daring.

Our house at Dillowie was massive. Parts of it were closed off and used as a kitchen for the shearers' cook. He prepared all the meals for the hardworking shearers.

It was a good thing he was there because I wouldn't have been able to cook for so many extra people! The shearers got morning tea, afternoon tea, supper, and three big meals a day. They were very well-fed men. If the shearers didn't like the cook's food, they simply stopped working until they got better meals.

I remember one time they went on strike because the cook made a stew they didn't enjoy. No one worked for three whole days! The owner had to hire a new cook before the shearing could continue.

Share-farming was never a path to wealth. At Parrakie, we battled against nature's whims - years too dry, too wet, with wheat withering and wool prices dropping lower than a lamb's tail. Ernie Hubble's property seemed to mock our efforts, each harvest a gamble we rarely won. But we adapted.

The property owner was a man named Emie Hubble from Adelaide. He only visited every couple of weeks to check on things. We attended the local Methodist church, where we became friends with the Byerlee family. Jack and Lila had four daughters then, and I think another child before we left.

Ted, Rae, and Bryce started at the tiny Geranium school in Parrakie. The boys liked it well enough, but poor Raelene had a tough start. I'll never forget the sadness on her face that first day. The teacher, Mr Verrall, told two girls to befriend her. But as soon as he looked away, the girls left Raelene standing alone by the wall. She seemed so small and lonely; it broke my heart. Thankfully, she made some true friends soon after.

We lived 14 miles out of town, and that's where I bravely learned to drive through deep sand. And now, guess what! There was another baby on the way.

Dinah and Biscuit were our two sweet milking cows back in Parrakie. Ted, Rae, Bryce, and even little Lesley took turns trying their hand at milking them. I can still picture Lel's rosy cheeks puffing out with effort as she pulled and tugged. The warm milk splashed into the pail, smelling of fresh hay and contentment. Those cows were among the few bright spots during our struggling days of share-farming.

The long drive to Lameroo felt like forever. My tummy was huge and tight. I couldn't wait to finally meet our new baby! Would it be a boy or a girl?

These last months have been so long, I thought, remembering the anticipation.

On April 15th, 1959, the doc said, "Get ready, it's time!" My heart raced like a rabbit. After many long hours, out came a tiny, pink bundle. A beautiful little girl!

"What a miracle," I whispered, cuddling her close. We named her Leonie Mavis - Leonie because it sounded so pretty, and Mavis after my Mum and me. She was finally here!

But the doc's face turned serious. "The cord was wrapped tightly around her neck. We almost lost her." My breath caught in my throat. I pulled Leonie closer, never wanting to let go.

How close we came to losing her, I would think later, my heart still racing at the memory.

While I was at the hospital, Mrs Simmons stayed with Ron and the other kids.

Mrs Simmons wasn't used to the countryside at all! One day, the kids took her on a walk through the scrubby fields near the house. But they got her all turned around on purpose. Poor Mrs Simmons couldn't find her way out! The kids thought it was hilarious, but she was scared.

Back at the hospital, I studied Leonie's perfect little features - her rosebud lips, button nose and chubby cheeks. She was absolute perfection. *Could there be any greater miracle than a new life?*

As the days passed, I marvelled at Leonie's every coo and wiggle. I was so grateful she arrived safely. That scary moment with the umbilical cord would be seared in my mind forever.

I made a silent vow to cherish each precious day with our sweet baby.

Can you imagine if we had lost her before even getting to know her? I shuddered at the thought. Leonie was a fighter, clearly destined to live a long, beautiful life.

I couldn't wait to have her home, snuggling in my arms and her Ron's big hugs. Our family felt complete.

Around that time, when Leonie was 6 months old, Ron and I decided we couldn't have any more babies. Back then, there wasn't birth control like "the pill." So, I had to get a special operation at the hospital. The doctor "cut and tied" my tubes to prevent more pregnancies.

While I was in the hospital for two whole weeks recovering, the Troubridge family lovingly cared for baby Leonie. They adored having her tiny self around.

But who watched our other kids? I couldn't rightly remember - maybe Mrs Simmons again? Or was it a Mrs Livingston? My memory wasn't the best even back then!

Lila Byerlee, a well-known person in the district, was known for always helping others in our small town. If someone had a problem, they called Lila. She opened her heart to everyone. But I guess the stress became too much.

One day, Lila's husband came home from working the fields. "Lila?" her husband called out. But she was nowhere to be found. He searched high and low, dread filling his chest. Finally, he saw the ladder leaning against the water tank...and the truth hit him like a ton of bricks. Poor Lila had climbed up and jumped in, ending her own life. We were all devastated.

How could someone so caring and needed be hurting that

deeply inside? It broke my heart into a million pieces. I'll never forget the gut-wrenching sadness on her husband's face when he told us the tragic news.

In December 1960, a dark cloud crept over our family. Ron's sweet mother - Nana Clark - passed away. As we huddled around her casket, saying our tear-stained goodbyes, did you ever imagine what lay ahead?

The following January, we bought Nana Clark's cosy house back in Edwardstown - a full circle homecoming.

The kids all started up at the same primary school that Ron attended as a child. Ted, Rae, Bryce and Lesley bounded through the halls and playground he knew like the back of his hand. Even Glenda joined them once she turned five, her baby curls bouncing alongside her siblings.

No more strangers' stares or feeling like outsiders! As I waved goodbye to my babies each morning, I couldn't help peeking across at the new building going up on Price Street. A warehouse by the look of those sturdy brick walls and smokestacks stretching toward the sky.

"What if that's a Tupperware warehouse?" I wondered aloud to Lee Puczkowski one day as we strolled to the shops together. She knew I longed for a steady job to finally bring in some reliable income.

Lee's eyes sparkled like she had an idea. "Why don't you go ask if they're hiring?"

My heart jumped into my throat. After all our struggles, could this be the lucky break we awaited? I opened my mouth to object, but Lee insisted on waiting while I inquired.

Before I could lose my courage, I marched right in and asked for an application.

The manager's smile stretched wider than the river itself. "Welcome aboard! We'll put you to work packing orders in the warehouse."

As I beamed brighter than a summer sun, dizziness and doubts swirled. Could I handle such hard labour after years as a homemaker? But Lee was right - this could be our chance. I deserved an opportunity to spread my wings.

That first gruelling week left my muscles screaming and my size six dress sagging looser than a saddlebag. But cashing that first hard-earned paycheck made every ache and pain worthwhile. Our family's luck was finally turning...

Or so I thought, until strange incidents started happening while I toiled away at the warehouse. Unexplainable events that knotted my insides tighter than a sailor's knots. Did someone have it out for me, or was I imagining the whispers and stares like a rattlesnake in the desert? Whatever was going on, I couldn't shake the ominous feeling that not every homecoming is celebrated with open arms.

Just when I thought our money worries were over, an icy chill ran down my spine at the warehouse.

Whose harsh glares pierced my back as I packed orders? What twisted lies were being whispered about me? I couldn't stop these thoughts.

CHAPTER 8

A Wrenching Decision

How does one rebuild after losing a life partner? What strength does it take to keep a family business alive when grief threatens to consume everything? My mother's story is a testament to resilience, hope, and unexpected grace.

It was just an ordinary Saturday when I visited my Stepdad, Ted, at the hospital. He'd been admitted a week earlier with another flare-up of his chronic stomach ulcer - an agonising condition he'd battled for years. Ted tried masking the searing pain by guzzling glasses of milk to coat his abused stomach lining. But this episode escalated far beyond his usual discomfort.

As I approached his room, raucous shouts echoed down the sterile hallway, sending a chill down my spine. That booming baritone could belong to only one person - my always-gentlemanly stepdad. I gasped, finding the nurses had actually strapped stepdad Ted to the bed like an unruly criminal to prevent his violent outbursts.

What cruel delusion or torturous pain warped his personality so severely? Seeing this proud, dignified man reduced to such an animalistic state shattered my heart into pieces.

The phone's harsh trill jolted me awake early the next morning - Sunday, July 18th, 1971. As soon as the hospital staff's grim words sank in, I recoiled as if physically struck by their impact. My beloved stepfather, who raised me as his very own, had peacefully slipped away alone sometime in the night.

My mind whirled with equal parts denial, sorrow, and panic. *How could someone so vital be gone forever? And how on earth could I possibly tell Mum that her cherished husband of over 30 years departed this world without her loving embrace?* The words became a lead weight lodged in my constricted throat.

Somehow, through my choked sobs, the awful truth tumbled out to my dear mother. We crumpled together on the sofa, our anguished wails echoing off the walls where Ted's larger-than-life presence still permeated every nook. For that soul-shattering moment, our family felt irreparably shattered too.

In the days and weeks that followed, our grief cycled between searing fresh and dull, like intermittent stabs to the heart.

After Dad's passing, Mum faced an enormous challenge. Their little shop, once a shared dream, now stood as a painful reminder of her loss. Yet she soldiered on, determined to keep their life's work afloat. Imagine a lone woman, managing every aspect of a small business while wrestling with profound grief - each day felt like rowing a fragile boat against crashing waves.

The daily grind proved too exhausting. With a heavy heart, she made the difficult decision to close the shop. But life, in its mysterious way, had another plan.

The Brighton Baptist Church emerged as an unexpected blessing. They took over the shop space, paying a modest rental fee to transform it into a quaint religious bookshop. While it wasn't the bustling business she and Dad had built, it offered Mum something equally precious: a sense of purpose and community precisely when she needed it most.

Picture her there - her smile warm, her hands lovingly arranging books, creating that charming shop atmosphere she had always cherished. This small nook amid book-lined walls became her comfort, like pulling on a well-worn, familiar sweater.

As years passed, her health declined. Eventually, she could no longer care for herself at home. With profound sadness, she made the wrenching decision to leave her cosy house behind, moving to Resthaven Nursing Home.

Her new room, with its kitchenette and private bath, offered independence. Yet I worried she seemed like a sweet little bird, fluttering alone in her cage. She mostly kept to herself, rarely socialising with other residents. Did she feel out of place, or simply cherish her hard-earned solitude? Some questions remain unanswered.

Dementia crept in slowly, like a quiet thief stealing her memories. Those tiny strokes robbed her of precise language, her once-fluid thoughts becoming fragmented. But through it all, her indomitable spirit remained brilliant. She may have forgotten my name some days, but never how to grace the world with her sunny smile.

She passed away on March 28th, 1990, as peacefully as she had lived. Her story teaches us that resilience isn't about never breaking. It's about finding the courage to rebuild, to adapt, and to discover purpose even in life's most challenging moments.

What does it mean to be a family when one partner is constantly on the move? Our story of Ron's travelling sales career reveals the delicate dance of maintaining connection and keeping a household running smoothly.

After moving to Edwardstown, Ron took a sales job with Wm. Haughton Company in Adelaide. His work demanded he be on the road from sunrise Monday through Friday evening. Our entire family's rhythm revolved around his weekly departures and returns.

The children and I would wait with bated breath, our hearts leaping each time his car pulled into the driveway. Was there any sweeter feeling than having Daddy back home? I probably anticipated his returns even more intensely than the kids.

Ron's smile was like plugging into pure happiness. No matter how exhausted I was from managing everything alone during the week, his bear hugs miraculously restored my strength. The children sensed my excitement, their faces lighting up brighter than a Halloween pumpkin's grin.

Our little home transformed from a cold, empty cabin to a warm, vibrant gathering place with Ron's presence. As his career progressed, he quickly advanced from a regular salesman to managing entire teams of representatives. His new responsibilities sometimes even included chaperoning work trips out of state for big conferences.

I can't help but chuckle now - with him gone so much, how did we ever find time to have six babies?

Ron's career trajectory coincided with significant national changes. February 1966 arrived with a revolutionary whisper - decimal currency was about to transform Australia. From the moment the government announced we'd be trading our familiar pounds and shillings for a sleek new monetary system, I felt excitement bubbling inside me.

Working at the Tupperware office, recently promoted to managing operations, I watched the country prepare for this monumental shift. Our shopping habits, schooling, and daily transactions would never be the same. The old coins - those weighty, clinking reminders of our colonial past - would soon become relics.

I remember imagining crowds at bank counters, trading handfuls of old currency for crisp new decimal notes. *Would it be chaotic? Confusing?* The conversions seemed daunting at first

- translating pounds, shillings, and pence into a rational metric system felt like learning an entirely new language.

But something magical happened. What seemed complex quickly became intuitive. Those first shiny coins, adorned with the Queen, a playful platypus, and quintessential Australian imagery, weren't just currency. They were a statement - a declaration of our nation's evolving identity, our resilience, our ability to adapt.

From my perch at Tupperware, I watched the transition unfold with wonder. Despite my initial fears of bureaucratic confusion, the change happened as smoothly as silk sliding through fingers. Little did I know that this year of national transformation would echo the personal changes brewing in our own family's story.

That same year brought unexpected challenges. While demonstrating equipment for Wm. Haughton, Ron, suffered a severe workplace accident. A heavy machine tumbled from its trailer, crashing onto his legs and breaking bones. The potential of amputation loomed like a dark cloud, but thankfully, multiple surgeries saved his leg.

His recovery was gruelling. Plaster encased his leg up to his hip, confining him to home for six endless weeks. I could still hear his muffled groans as he tried adjusting his position on the couch. Yet, Ron's unbreakable spirit prevailed. Even when he suffered another setback, shattering his ankle during his return to work, his perseverance remained undiminished.

This resilience ultimately led us to our greatest adventure - founding our own company, Haughton Honda, after Wm.

Haughton shut down their Adelaide operations. What began as a challenging transition became our most significant professional and personal journey.

Our partnership was never just about surviving; it was about thriving together, supporting each other through every twist and turn life presented.

I was still juggling my Tupperware responsibilities, I remembered, *carefully balancing my existing commitments with this audacious dream of launching our own business.* The early days of Haughton Honda were a delicate dance of hope and hard work. By 1978, our long-deferred dreams had finally bloomed into reality.

Our tight-knit team became our strength. Year after year, we hit sales targets that seemed almost impossible. The competition was fierce, but Ron's unwavering passion for Honda kept us moving forward. *Each sale was more than a transaction,* I would often think.

The seemingly impossible happened - an all-expenses-paid trip to Japan emerged as our grand prize. *Can you imagine our excitement?* The memory still brings a rush of emotion.

Stepping off the plane into the Land of the Rising Sun was like entering a different world. The culture, tranquil gardens, and exotic delicacies were breathtaking. Ron's connection to Japan, sparked during his WWII deployment, came alive in every moment.

I caught myself stealing glances at Ron, watching his face light up with childlike wonder. While gracefully navigating the ordered chaos, our senses delighted in every glimpse of the brilliant red terracotta shrines, meticulously manicured gardens, and bustling urban crossroads, melding rich heritage with modern flair. In those moments, my chest swelled with profound gratitude that after enduring such gut-wrenching loss, we embarked on this grand adventure together as loving partners.

These trips were more than just business rewards. They were adventures that drew us closer together, forging friendships with locals that would last a lifetime. We had tea ceremonies, did traditional dances and shared meals at Kiku restaurant's known for its exquisite delicacies, with Army comrades who had fallen in love with Japanese brides.

But business is never a straight path. As other Japanese companies flooded the market with tempting new products, our position became increasingly precarious. Ron's fierce brand loyalty - a trait I both admired and worried about - began to show its limitations.

Watching our market share dwindle was like witnessing a slow-motion tragedy, I reflected. Competitors chipped away at our business, and our sales reduced to a mere trickle. The writing was on the wall, and we knew it.

In 1987, we made the heart-wrenching decision to put our dream up for sale. *How do you let go of something that's been your entire world?* The business bearing our family's name was more than just a company - it was our shared vision, our collective heartbeat.

But Ron's spirit remained unbroken. *If anything, this was just another adventure,* he would say, his eyes twinkling with that familiar determination. We decided to shake things up completely - selling not just the business, but our old house as well, since the kids were grown and long gone at the time.

Woodcroft became our new home - a sun-dappled community that slowly transformed from a barren park to a bustling neighbourhood. Our new home became more than an address. It became the heartwarming hub that drew our family together.

Lel and Tich and their two children, Shane and Kymberly, lived practically next door. Glenda's crew with Neil, Julie, and Kerry were just a skip away too. Same with Leonie's family alongside Allen, Danni, and Amy.

✿

Yet Ted's incredible faith, instilled through numerous life trials, inspired us to pick up the shattered pieces and carry on.

While our family increased through the years as the kids grew up and moved away to chase their own dreams, the door was always open for grandchildren to race through. I can vividly picture their squeals of delight chasing each other through those grassy yards Ron meticulously manicured like the greenskeeper for a prestigious country club. Watching Ron's cheeky grin and bright eyes light up as the little ones clambered onto his lap reminded me so much of his softer side.

I would swell with so much pride as I flitted between hosting marathon colouring sessions or tea parties to chatting with whichever daughter or daughter-in-law dropped by, I couldn't help but swell with immense pride. Our humble new digs steadily blossomed into the cheerful epicentre for making wonderful memories together as a multi-generational family.

While Ron flourished, keeping every minute purposefully crammed, I opted for a slightly more relaxed pace. My hands stayed busy with various craft projects, sure, but the computer quickly became my favourite hobby. Losing myself in those digital realms provided such a welcome escape from, well, everything else.

The quiet hum of the computer became my refuge. After years of bustling family life, of hosting gatherings and supporting Ron's endless community activities, I discovered a different kind of joy in these digital spaces. It wasn't about being productive or serving others - it was about finding a moment just for myself.

Sometimes, I'd catch Ron glancing at me, his eyebrow slightly raised, watching me navigate these new digital landscapes. He never quite understood my fascination, but he respected it. That was Ron - always supportive, always giving me the space to explore my own interests.

Craft projects still littered our kitchen table - half-finished embroideries, sketches, bits of coloured paper. But the computer? It was different. It was a window to worlds I'd never imagined, a quiet adventure where I could be entirely myself, without the constant demands of family, community, and caregiving.

※

Speaking of unexpected detours, perhaps I should elaborate on my little stroke incident back in 1994? I nearly glossed over it completely because, thankfully, it wasn't too severe in the grand scheme. Can you believe I consciously ignored those frightening symptoms for two full days before finally caving and informing the family?

Ron, wonderfully overprotective as ever, didn't dare waste another second before jolting into crisis mode. His frantic phone call for emergency help still rings in my ears all these years later. I can vividly picture the panic etching grooves around his baby blues as the ambulance crew whisked me away to Flinders Medical Centre.

While the doctors poked and prodded with various tests, I maintained my usual plucky front. A couple of aspirin per day, and I'd be right as rain before you knew it! Except they insisted on sending me home to simply wait and see how things progressed from there. Yes, wait and see if I lived or died without any further treatment.

Ron and I exchanged bewildered looks. Had the so-called medical experts lost their minds along with their compassion? I couldn't decipher whether indignant fury or gut-wrenching fear knotted my insides more tightly.

Squeezing my clammy hand, Ron donned his most reassuring

tone. "Don't fret, love. We're not just going to sit idly by if this is truly as bad as it seems." With a determined glint flickering behind his eyes, he ushered me into the car and peeled out of the parking lot like a bat out of you-know-where.

Before I could fully process the frenzied events whirling around me, Ron deposited me at our familiar local practitioner's office. Dear Dr Ward's concern instantly melted into resolute action, he cut through the bureaucratic nonsense like a hot knife through butter.

Within the hour, I found myself setting up semi-permanent residency in a cosy room at the Vale's private hospital. The expert care enveloped me like being swaddled in warm, downy blankets - Dr Ward's daily visits, the physiotherapists gently guiding me through exercises, soothing words and smiles all around.

Yet even as my wobbly limbs gradually regained strength and feeling over those eight long days, an ominous cloud still hovered overhead. What came next would forever determine if I beat those staggering odds or fell victim to an even crueller fate.

CHAPTER 9

Commemorating Ted's Divine Moments

They say a mother's memory works like a camera roll—capturing every first smile, every milestone, every precious moment. I left the hospital holding thirteen days of motherhood in my trembling hands and a lifetime of worry in my heart.

"Mrs Clark?" The nurse's voice was gentle but firm. "We're dreadfully overbooked with this post-war baby boom. Would you be able to leave a day early if you have family to stay with?"

Oh Lord, I'm not ready, my heart screamed silently. But outwardly, I managed a weak smile. "Yes, I can stay with my parents."

After confirming I could temporarily move in with Mum and Dad, the nurses immediately shifted me upstairs to clear my bed. Suddenly, I found myself isolated in a private room, tears streaming down my cheeks as reality set in.

That night, alone in the private room upstairs, I cradled my son (Ronald Edwin Junior, whom we nicknamed Ted) close. "What do I know about being your mummy?" I whispered to his sleeping face. "I hope I don't mess this up, little one."

As unease twisted my stomach into knots, I couldn't wait to be discharged the following morning into my mother's experienced, loving arms.

Auntie Viv's arrival the next morning brought welcome relief. "Look at this precious bundle!" she cooed, expertly scooping him into her arms. "He's absolutely perfect, Carol. You've done magnificently."

Perfect doesn't mean I know what I'm doing, I thought, but her confidence was contagious.

I'll never forget gazing down at his perfect rosebud lips and cherubic face nestled against me with starry-eyed wonder. A new grandchild signified hope and boundless love blossoming from the ashes of World War II's devastation.

At Mum's flat, reality crashed in like a tidal wave. "I can't remember which end the nappy goes on!" I wailed one particularly overwhelming morning.

Mum's laugh tinkled like wind chimes as she demonstrated for the hundredth time. "I said the exact same thing with you. Trust me, one day you'll do this in your sleep."

"In my sleep?" I snorted. "That's if I ever sleep again!"

Her warm hand squeezed my shoulder. "You're doing just

beautifully. We'll get the hang of this routine together."

Whenever Ted achieved a milestone, you can bet we cheered louder than at the World Cup finals.

One afternoon, I'll never forget giddily seizing Ted under the armpits in his Granddad's sitting room, waiting with bated breath for him to work his magic.

My dad, baby Ted's granddad, barely had time to blink before a veritable torrent sprayed forth - bullseye into his freshly brewed cuppa! As the brown liquid rapidly dampened his moustache, he fixed me with an incredulous look.

All I could do was giggle sheepishly while fumbling for a dishtowel.

"Right, that's it for fancy teatime around these parts!" Granddad bellowed, his moustache twitching in wounded dignity.

Those blissful, bonding weeks flew far too quickly before Ron's deployment ended, and it was time to set off on our own again.

Yet even as I tearfully said goodbye to the cosy familiarity of home, I clutched Ted close, knowing our greatest adventure still awaited.

The first asthma attack struck without warning. Ted's tiny chest heaved as panic gripped my own.

"Ron!" My voice cracked with terror. "Something's wrong with the baby!"

Please breathe, please breathe, became my silent prayer through countless nights of vigilance. Each wheeze felt like a knife to my heart.

The Vicks VapoRub incident stands out in sharp relief. "It might help his breathing," Ron suggested, reaching for the jar, and he rubbed it on his chest to help open his airways. Big mistake! The strong menthol fumes only made the situation worse as Ted's gasping intensified.

"The bath! Get him in the bath!" I commanded, already running the water. As steam filled the bathroom, I held my precious boy close. "I'm so sorry, my darling," I whispered to him. Thank goodness, the bath did the trick, and he slowly stabilised.

From then on, we treaded very carefully around any home remedies or vapour treatments. The littlest thing could trigger another life-threatening asthma attack in our fragile son. It broke my heart seeing him suffer so mightily just to inhale and exhale.

After consulting specialist after specialist with no success, someone recommended trying a naturopath named Mr Human. *What if this makes things worse? What if this is our only hope?*

"What have we got to lose?" Ron said, reading my thoughts as he often did.

Miraculously, his natural treatments seemed to finally break the vicious asthma cycle! Over the next couple of months, Ted's crushing episodes gradually diminished from weeks to days to disappearing altogether.

The day Ted took his first clear breath in weeks, I couldn't hold back my tears. "Look at him, Ron! Listen to how quiet his breathing is!" We remained eternally grateful. Mr Human helped our Teddy overcome his biggest childhood battle.

"You're a fighter, my Ted," I whispered that night, watching him sleep peacefully. "And you've taught Mummy to be one too."

However, the respiratory issues morphed into different symptoms like hay fever and allergies as he grew older. I suppose trading one struggle for another wasn't ideal, but at least this allowed him to breathe freely again.

Like the shifting sands of the Australian outback, our family's journey took us from town to town across South Australia, each move bringing new challenges and opportunities for young Ted. In retrospect, I see how these constant changes, while daunting at the time, helped forge the resilient spirit that would define his character.

I remember his hair sticking up in every direction on those early mornings, rubbing the sleep from his eyes and protesting about having to get ready so early.

But soon enough, that grumpy pout melted into excited grins as he raced out the door to join his new classmates.

His too-big uniform practically swimming on his small frame as he clutched his leather satchel with white-knuckled determination. The night before, he'd laid out everything just so – even his pencils arranged in perfect rows. That's the thing about children; they create their own order in the face of change.

"Mum, did you see how high up we are?" Ted gasped when we first arrived at Maitland on the Yorke Peninsula. The salty air and open skies were a far cry from the sheltered hills of

Woodside. Yet Ted, like many children facing change, found his footing quickly.

When work took us to the sheep station outside Jamestown, Ted found himself at Whyte Yarcowie Area School. "It's like having one big family instead of separate classes," he explained one evening, helping me with the dishes. The one-room schoolhouse might have seemed a step backward to some, but it offered lessons you couldn't find in any textbook.

I'd often find myself standing at the kitchen window, tea in hand, watching him race across the paddocks with the other children. "Just look at them go," I'd murmur to myself, their laughter carried on the wind as they invented games among the sheep yards and eucalyptus trees. Those were the moments that made all the moving worthwhile.

The transition to Geranium school in Parrakie brought its own challenges. By seventh grade, Ted was starting to show the first signs of adolescence. "Mum, do I really have to wear these pants? They're too short again!" became a common morning refrain. But even as his voice cracked and his limbs grew gangly, his ability to adapt remained steadfast.

"But Mum, everyone uses the back streets!" Ted had protested when I gave him strict instructions about his cycling route to school. That teenage sense of invincibility led to a nasty spill, of course. As I cleaned his scraped knees and elbows, I couldn't help but smile a bit. "I suppose this means I was right about those 'safe' shortcuts?" I teased gently, earning a sheepish grin in return.

Perhaps the biggest change came with the decision to send Ted to Brighton to live with Nana and Granddad Hulbert for high school. "You'll be just fine," I assured him, though my heart was doing somersaults. The bustling suburbs of Adelaide were a world away from the quiet rural life he'd known.

Those years with Nana and Granddad Hulbert shaped Ted in ways we couldn't have predicted. Every afternoon, Nana would have her ritual ready. "Come on then, love," she'd say, patting the kitchen chair beside her. "Tell your old Nan all about your day." She had a way of making even the most mundane day sound like an adventure worth telling.

When Nana's health began to fail, it marked the end of an era. I can still hear her voice, weak but determined: "Promise me you'll look after my house, dear. It needs a family to keep its heart beating." Her passing in late 1960 left a void that seemed impossible to fill. Yet even in grief, our family found a way forward. Taking over the Edwardstown home wasn't just about having a place to live; it was about honouring Nana's memory and finally putting down roots after years of wandering.

"You know," I often tell my grandchildren now, "your father learned more from all those school changes than just reading and sums." Looking back at those years of transition, I'm struck by how each move, each new school, each challenge helped shape not just Ted's education, but his character.

Children, I've learned, are like young saplings – they bend with the wind, growing stronger and more resilient with each battle they fight. Ted's journey through multiple schools wasn't just about academic learning; it was about discovering that home isn't just a place – it's the people who help you grow, the memories you make along the way, and the strength you find within yourself to embrace change.

❁

Life rarely follows the straight path we envision for ourselves. Ted's journey from aspiring teacher to banker to military officer perfectly illustrates how unexpected turns often lead us to exactly where we're meant to be.

"Mum, I've been thinking," Ted said one evening over dinner, fidgeting with his napkin. "I'm not sure teaching is really what I want to do." My heart gave a little flutter – that Education Department grant (a generous 50-pound grant, about $100 back then, to help cover his studies) had seemed like such a blessing. But watching him struggle with the decision, I knew he needed support, not judgment.

"Better to realise it now than after years in the classroom," I told him, though privately I worried about repaying those fifty pounds. Ted's relief at my response was worth every penny we'd have to scrape together.

The banking sector was booming in those days, offering bright young people opportunities for advancement. When Ted applied to several banks, he came home practically buzzing with excitement. "Four of them, Mum! Four banks want me!" His face lit up as he waved the acceptance letters, including one from the Bank of New South Wales.

I remember the morning in 1965 when Ted first headed off to the Bank of New South Wales, his father's old tie carefully knotted at his throat. "You look every inch the banker," I'd said, straightening his collar while blinking back proud tears.

Those early days weren't easy – no computers back then to help balance the books. Many nights, I'd hear him come in late, his footsteps heavy with exhaustion. "Sorry, I'm so late, Mum," he'd call out. "The till was off by three pence, and I had to find it." I'd warm up his dinner, listening to stories about the day's transactions and demanding customers.

When the Port Lincoln position opened up, Ted's eyes sparkled with possibility. The bank manager pulled us aside, his brow furrowed with concern. "Mrs Clark, is everything alright at home?" he asked carefully. "Oh goodness, yes!" I couldn't help but laugh. "Our Ted just wants to spread his wings a bit."

Then came the National Service lottery. I remember standing in the kitchen, hands trembling as I held the newspaper, searching for Ted's birthdate among those chosen. His marble wasn't drawn – but that evening, he made an announcement that stopped us in our tracks.

"I'm going to volunteer anyway," he said quietly over dinner. Ron's fork paused halfway to his mouth, and I felt my heart skip a beat. "Are you sure, son?" his father asked. Ted's response was simple but determined: "Yes, Dad. It's the right thing to do."

What came next still fills me with pride when I think about it. After basic training, a letter arrived announcing his selection for Officers' Training School at Scheyville. "My boy, an officer!" Ron kept saying, his chest puffed out with pride. I tried to focus on that pride instead of my worry as we prepared to send our son off to Victoria.

Nine months later, watching him receive his commission as a 2nd Lieutenant, I hardly recognised the confident young man in uniform. "You've done us proud, Ted," Ron whispered, his voice rough with emotion, as we embraced our son after the ceremony.

Papua New Guinea seemed a world away when Ted was posted there with the 2nd Battalion Pacific Island Regiment. His letters home painted pictures of dense jungles and exotic landscapes. "The humidity is like nothing you've ever experienced, Mum," he wrote. "Makes an Adelaide summer feel like a spring breeze!"

His 21st birthday was the hardest – our boy becoming a man so far from home. We arranged to call him at the base in Wewak. "Having a proper celebration, son?" I asked, trying to keep my voice steady across the crackling connection. "The boys have arranged something special, Mum," he assured me, sounding so grown up. "Though nothing beats your birthday cakes."

"Would you believe it?" I told our neighbours proudly, showing them the newspaper article about Ted's achievements. "From bank teller to army officer in just a few years!" Carefully clipping that article, I thought about all the twists and turns that had led him here.

In retrospect, I see how each decision, each pivot in Ted's

journey, built upon the last. "Sometimes the long way round is the right way there," as my mother used to say. Ted's early career proves just that – success isn't about sticking to the original plan, it's about having the courage to forge your own way.

❁

It was actually through Ted's work connections that he crossed paths with the woman who would become his wife. In 1970, Ted met a young lady named Josephine Mary Fryar, though everyone called her Jo.

She had been living in Canberra but was back visiting family that June long weekend. As fate would have it, they attended the same party and immediately hit it off.

It turns out that Jo's brothers, Glen and Neville, both worked at the bank, so Ted already knew them before meeting their sister that night.

We first laid eyes on Jo ourselves when Ted excitedly brought her home after an evening out together and introduced her right at our bedroom door!

The romance blossomed quickly from there. By that September, Ted and Jo were engaged. They became husband and wife that December in a lovely ceremony at Westminster Chapel on the Westminster College campus in Marion.

Jo had one girlfriend serve as her bridesmaid, while our daughter Raelene filled the other bridesmaid role. Raelene's little girl, Karen, even got to be the precious flower girl. They all looked so beautiful in their sunny yellow dresses!

Jo came from a wonderful family, including her brother Barry, who has Down syndrome. While her parents have sadly passed away now, Barry resides full-time at Minda Home under his siblings' caring watch on the weekends.

Once married, Jo transferred back to Adelaide and landed a job at the Commonwealth Employment Office while the newlyweds settled into a flat in Unley. The year 1971 also marked another milestone when Ted proudly purchased his first brand-new car - a shiny Toyota Corona.

Every family's story has its pivotal chapters, and for Ted and Jo, 1972 marked the beginning of their most important one. I still catch my breath thinking about that phone call announcing Adam Joseph's arrival at Ashford Hospital. There's something almost sacred about becoming a grandmother – watching your own child step into parenthood. In that moment, I saw time fold in on itself, remembering my own first days with Ted.

"She did all the work, of course," Ted said sheepishly when showing off his newborn son. "I was just there for moral support." But the pride in his voice told a different story. Jo, exhausted but radiant, simply smiled and squeezed his hand. *Strange how the smallest hands can make the strongest hearts,* I thought, watching Adam's tiny fingers wrap around Ted's thumb.

Life has a way of keeping young parents on their toes. I remember the mixture of pride and anxiety in Ted's voice when he announced his promotion to 2nd Officer at the Jamestown branch. "It's not a big operation," he explained, bouncing Adam on his knee, "but it's a step up."

Sometimes the biggest blessings come wrapped in the smallest packages, I mused as I watched Jo efficiently pack up their life once again. She had a quiet strength about her that reminded me of myself at her age – facing each new challenge with grace and determination.

The move to Renmark in 1973 felt different somehow. Perhaps it was the way the Murray River seemed to embrace the town, its steady flow a reminder that life, like water, finds its own path. Their little bank house on 16th Street became more than just a residence; it became the stage for their growing family's story.

It's funny how friendship works, I realised, watching the Warrens and the Chigros family become part of their extended family. Chester and Val, John and Di – they weren't just neighbours anymore. They were becoming the village that every young family needs. Some nights, sitting on their veranda and listening to the chorus of laughter and conversation, I'd think to myself. *This is what community means – hearts connecting over shared moments and simple joys.*

Then came that magical December 19th, 1973 – their third wedding anniversary and the day Bevan Heath made his appearance. Once again, the doting husband was right by Jo's side as she did the hard labour.

"Well, this is certainly one way to celebrate!" Ted joked through happy tears. *Life has its own perfect timing,* I thought, watching their family expand in both numbers and love.

Those brown eyes of Bevan's – oh, how they sparked conversations! In our fair-haired, blue-eyed family, they were like a beautiful plot twist in our genetic story. *Perhaps, I pondered, this is nature's way of reminding us that every child brings their own unique gifts to the family.*

The toilet training adventures! Modern parenting has certainly changed from my day. Watching Ted and Jo celebrate each small victory with such enthusiasm made me realise something important: *Sometimes the greatest progress comes not from pushing forward, but from pausing to celebrate the small steps.*

Watching Jo navigate motherhood brought back so many memories. During our quiet chats, she'd confess, "I feel like I'm making it up as I go along." *Aren't we all?* I thought. *That's the beautiful secret of parenting – we grow alongside our children.*

Ted's dedication to fatherhood touched my heart in unexpected ways. Seeing him rush home for bath time, his banker's composure giving way to playful splashes and baby giggles, I realised something beautiful: *Our children don't just make us parents; they make us more fully human.*

Those years in Renmark were more than just a chapter in their lives; they were a transformation. Each diaper changed, each promotion celebrated, each friendship forged was a thread in our family story. *Perhaps that's the real miracle of family life,* I often think now, *how the ordinary moments weave together to create something extraordinary.*

Subsequently, I realised how each challenge and triumph shaped them not just as parents but as people. In the midst of midnight feedings, career decisions, community building, and childhood milestones, they were writing their own definition of home—and what a beautiful definition it turned out to be.

CHAPTER 10

Ducky Ride Became a Nightmare

The murky waters of the River Murray held many secrets, but none quite like the morning our rubber ducky boat left us stranded between dawn and breakfast, testing both our arms and our spirits. Lord, give me strength, I thought as I watched the propeller sink into those dark waters. While Ted diligently studied for his accountancy certificate at TAFE, the rest of us delighted in lazy summer holidays near the river.

Ron and I frequently towed our little caravan to the Renmark holiday park, setting up camp for weeks at a time over Christmas breaks. *This is what memories are made of,* I'd think to myself, watching the sunset paint the river gold. That humble rubber ducky of ours provided endless hours of simple joy, peddling around the main river and winding backwater channels.

All the regulars at the caravan park knew us by that little boat's signature presence. *Funny how a silly rubber boat can become part of who you are,* I'd muse as we'd wave to familiar faces along the shore. We built such warm friendships with the other families who returned year after year - there's something special about sharing lazy days by the river that brings people together.

I remember one particular morning when we roused a very sleepy Shane from his bunk and plopped him into the ducky before the sun was even up. *Perhaps we should have let the poor dear sleep,* I thought guiltily, watching him yawn. Like a tribe of adventurous ducklings, we merrily set off to explore those glassy, predawn waters while the world still slumbered.

Well, wouldn't you know it - in a blink, our tranquil voyage turned to chaos when the propeller suddenly disconnected and sank to the murky depths! *Oh, brilliant. Just brilliant,* I remember thinking as we floated helplessly. There we were, stranded in the middle of the vast river with no choice but to start rowing with our bare arms back towards the distant shore. *Next time I suggest an early morning boat ride, someone please stop me,* I silently grumbled as my arms began to ache.

Sweat poured, empty bellies growled, and little Shane innocently wondered when he'd ever get breakfast as we struggled against the lazy current's resistance. *If we ever make it back,* I thought, *I'm cooking up the biggest breakfast this family's ever seen.* By the time our exhausted party finally dragged the ducky ashore at the caravan park, Jo and Ted were frantic with worry over our mysterious disappearance.

The year 1976 brought exciting changes for our family. After three wonderful years in Renmark, Ted got a transfer back to Adelaide as a Senior Instructor at the bank's Wales Training Centre. *Change is good,* I kept telling myself. They bought a cosy home in Glengowrie to start this new chapter.

1977 proved to be a truly momentous year full of changes. In February, their firstborn, Adam, reached the big milestone of starting school and weeks later, Ted made a bold move to leave banking and join the Fruit Co-op over in Berri instead. *Renmark wasn't done with them yet.* While getting situated, he stayed with our dear friends, the Warren and Chigros families, for about six weeks each. Those families were such a blessing - the kind of friends who become like family.

That May, he sold their Glengowrie house and moved back to Renmark. At first, he rented the Church Manse on 14th Street while he worked on something more permanent - a kit home which they were building on Tapio Street. By September, they'd started construction, and come November, they moved in even though it was only 70% complete!

That first winter was interesting, I can tell you. They spent their evenings and weekends putting the finishing touches on the rooms themselves, gradually turning that skeleton of a house into a proper home. The Warren and Chigros families were right there with them through it all, lending a hand whenever they needed it. Their children would play with Ted's while the adults worked on the house, turning their building site into quite the community gathering spot.

Living in Renmark shaped their family in ways I never expected. The rhythm of life there was different - measured by river levels and fruit seasons rather than city schedules. Even when Ted's work changed again in 1978, the town's spirit kept them grounded.

As I now understand, I can't help but smile at how that 70% complete house mirrored their own journey - a work in progress that turned out better than any perfect, ready-made home could have been. *Sometimes, I realise now, the best things in life start out unfinished.* The River Murray kept flowing, marking time as our family grew and changed, but those Renmark years will always hold a special place in our hearts.

❀

The following year, 1978, marked young Bevan's turn to start school too. Ted resigned from the Fruit Co-op, bought a boat, and launched a new charter business instead. His wife, Jo, took a job at the Renmark Country Club as well. While Ted's boating venture only lasted until 1979, that same year, he pivoted into a rewarding role as the Administrative Manager of the Riverland TAFE College. Jo transitioned to employment at the Renmano Wines company during this period, too.

Ted also achieved a major accomplishment by finally completing his accountancy studies and beginning to teach part-time at TAFE.

Throughout the early 80s, their careers remained in flux. Jo worked stints at the Renmark Medical Centre in 1983, with Ted becoming a Finance Officer at E&WS in Berri the next year. He also juggled volunteer gigs like the Renmark Tourist Office in this season of life.

Of course, the highest points remained watching their sons, Adam and Bevan, flourish and embrace incredible opportunities.

1991 stands out in my memory like a photograph catching the sun just right. The day Adam's scholarship letter arrived, I must have read it ten times over. *University of Adelaide... full academic scholarship... distinguished achievement...* I imagine this achievement fueled Ted and Jo's decision to relocate the family back to the city in the coming years. When Ted landed that position with SA Water in Adelaide in 1993, it felt meant to be.

With Bevan also beginning university studies around then, they sold their Renmark home as well as the beloved boat and purchased a new house in the Edwardstown suburb. As the boys embraced these new education paths, Jo secured employment with Hyde Park Press.

Before long, Adam departed for Melbourne to start his career - but not before meeting a special lady named Paula Cook. Talk about life moving quickly!

Bevan's path took a different turn that nearly gave us grey hair. "I'm leaving university," he announced one evening over dinner. My fork clattered against the plate. *Deep breaths,* I told myself, while my mind raced with worries about his future. But watching him work and save money, I began to see a different kind of determination in his eyes. *Maybe university isn't the only path to success,* I'd think, noting how he studied travel books the way his brother had studied calculus.

❖

Then came Adam's Melbourne announcement. "It's a great career opportunity," he explained, but all I could think was *Melbourne might as well be the moon.* I put on my brave mother face and helped him pack, slipping his favourite childhood photos into his suitcase when he wasn't looking. *He'll want these someday,* I told myself, though really, I needed to know a piece of home was going with him.

Life has a way of surprising you, though. Soon, Adam was calling about this lovely girl named Paula he'd met. I could hear the smile in his voice, and suddenly Melbourne didn't seem so far away. *My boy's found love,* I thought, and the worry in my heart started making room for joy.

Not to be outdone, Bevan came home one day practically floating. "Her name is Joanne," he said, and I recognised that look - the same one his father had worn when we were young. Before we knew it, they were planning their world tour together. *There goes my baby,* I thought, watching them pore over maps and guidebooks, *but oh, what adventures they'll have.*

Ron and I couldn't bear sitting still while our children explored the world. In 1997, we traced their footsteps across continents - Japan, England, Scotland, the Netherlands, and Germany. Meeting the families who'd hosted our boys brought everything full circle. *They have more than one family now,* I realised, seeing how these people from across the globe had taken our children into their hearts.

The proudest - and most surprising - moment came in 1998 when Bevan announced he was returning to university. *He needed to find his own way back,* I thought, watching him tackle his studies with new determination. When he landed that job with Australian Unity in 2000, I wasn't even surprised anymore that it was in Melbourne. *Both my birds in the same distant nest, I mused, looking after each other.*

Standing in Adam and Paula's wedding in March 2000, I found myself remembering a thousand little moments: Adam learning to tie his shoes, skinned knees I'd kissed better, report cards proudly displayed on the fridge. *When did my little boy become this confident man?* Now here he was, starting his own family, and my heart felt like it might burst.

By 2001, when Ted and Jo were exploring Thailand's northern mysteries, I had finally learned to embrace the space between holding tight and letting go. *Our children are our greatest adventure,* I thought one evening, watching the sun set over ancient temples. They'd flown further than we ever dreamed, but their wings had grown strong in our nest. And isn't that exactly what we hoped for, all those years ago?

Sitting here today, looking through our old photo albums, I can't help but think how much our family's story resembles the Murray itself. *Like the river,* I thought, touching a faded photograph of our rubber ducky boat, *we've had our calm stretches and our rapids.*

That old river taught us more than we realised at the time. When our propeller sank into those murky waters that dawn morning, leaving us stranded with hungry children and aching arms, we learned to laugh at life's little disasters. *Sometimes you just have to row harder and trust you'll reach shore,* I'd tell myself during tough times. The river knew what it was teaching us all along.

Looking at pictures of our half-built house on Tapio Street makes me smile now. *Were we brave or just naive?* I wonder, remembering how we moved in with only 70% complete walls around us. But that's how life works, isn't it? You start with something unfinished and build it together, just like we did with that kit home. Ted and I didn't know then that we were showing our children how to embrace uncertainty, how to build something from scratch with your own two hands.

The Murray's seen it all - our little ones splashing in its shallows, then growing into teenagers who'd rather sleep in than join our dawn expeditions. Now Adam and Bevan have their own families, their own adventures far from its banks. *But the river's still part of their story, I realise, flowing through their memories like it flows through our land.*

When Adam got his scholarship and Bevan set off to travel the world, I'd sometimes walk down to the river's edge and watch its steady current. *Keep flowing, keep moving forward,* it seemed to whisper, even on days when my heart ached from missing them. That same river that once cradled our rubber ducky now carries our grandchildren when they visit, their laughter echoing across the water just like their parents' did.

The Murray taught us about change, too. Some years it floods, others it barely trickles, but it never stops moving. Just like our family - through job changes, moves, marriages, and Melbourne adventures, we've kept flowing forward. *Life doesn't let you stay in one eddy for too long,* I've learned. Ted's career shifted like the river's course, from banking to fruit co-ops to boats to education. Each bend brought new challenges, new views, new reasons to be grateful.

Sometimes I wonder what the river remembers of us all. Those summer evenings when the Warren and Chigros families would gather on its banks, sharing meals and dreams while our children played in the shallows. The morning Ted and I sold our beloved boat, both crying a little as we watched it motor away with its new owners. *The river holds our memories, I think, keeps them safe in its depths like treasures.*

Now our grandchildren ask about the river stories - about the time we got stranded, about building our home, about their parents growing up on these banks. Their eyes shine with the same wonder I once saw in their parents' eyes. *The river's magic hasn't changed,* I realise, *even if we have.*

They say home is where the heart is, but I think sometimes home is where your stories begin. Ours started with that rubber ducky boat and a half-built house, with dawn adventures and community suppers, with children who grew up to be braver than we ever imagined. The Murray's are still flowing, still teaching new generations about patience and persistence, about taking risks and finding your way home again.

Like the river, I think, watching our grandchildren skip stones across its surface, *our family's story has no end - it just keeps flowing, gathering new tributaries, finding new paths forward.* And isn't that the greatest gift we could have given our children? Not just a house by the river, but the courage to follow their own current, knowing they'll always have a shore to return to.

CHAPTER 11

Bold Notes: Daughters' Symphony

The first time my daughter Raelene got behind the wheel of a car at age twenty-five, I held my breath. Unlike her siblings, who learned from their father Ron's patient instruction, Raelene had waited until 1974 to spread her wings on the open road. Perhaps it was fitting - my free-spirited daughter had always done things in her own time, on her own terms.

Her first taste of the working world came at a real estate office on South Road in Black Forest around 1965. The secretarial position proved short-lived - after just three weeks, she'd had enough! "I simply can't spend another day filing papers," she announced one evening, and that was that.

Her next role brought her to Badenoch's Transport, where she worked as secretary to the accountant. That position lasted longer, though she often complained about one particularly annoying coworker who seemed to take great delight in flicking paper clips at her every time she walked past his desk. "One of these days," she'd mutter under her breath, "those paper clips are going right back at him."

1974 brought significant change when Raelene started working at Levi's, making jeans. It was here that fate played its hand - she met Margaret Scott, who had a son named Chris. Little did we know then how that connection would shape her future. The job at Levi's seemed to give her confidence, and between 1977 and 1985, she explored various positions, even travelling to America once or twice for work. These experiences broadened her horizons and eventually led her toward a career in banking at Westpac.

But it was music that first truly captured Raelene's heart and showed us her adventurous spirit. At seventeen, she made an announcement that caught us completely off guard - she wanted to learn the bagpipes! "I know it sounds strange," she said, seeing our surprised faces, "but I just have to try." Now, we didn't know anyone else who played such an instrument, but we supported her unconventional choice wholeheartedly. Soon enough, she joined the S.A. Ladies' Highland Pipe Band, where she flourished in ways we never expected.

Her natural talent with the pipes became evident when, after just three months of practice, she was selected to compete with the band in Perth. That trip nearly ended in disaster before it began! I'll never forget the moment the train pulled out of Adelaide station in 1966, and I realised with horror that I still had her handbag containing her ticket and every dollar she needed for the journey. *Lord help me,* I thought, *how am I going to fix this?* With Ron laid up with a broken leg, I had to make a mad dash in our old car to Balaklava station, 60 miles away. The stationmaster had radioed ahead to slow the train, and by some miracle, I managed to throw her bag to the guard just in time. When she returned home with her medals and accolades, she just shook her head and laughed about her parents' frantic efforts to make sure she could compete. The bagpipes brought such joy to our family that her sisters eventually joined the band too, taking up the drums.

Like many young hearts seeking adventure, Raelene set her sights on joining the Navy in November 1967. But before she donned her sailor's uniform, she'd met a young man named Christopher Parry. Though they weren't officially engaged during her brief military service, their connection remained strong. *History does have a way of repeating itself,* I thought, watching her struggle with military life just as I had in my youth. Within months, she requested a discharge to return home, where her heart truly belonged. "Some dreams," she told me later, "aren't quite what we imagine them to be."

Back in Adelaide, her romance with Christopher blossomed into something more permanent. In April 1968, they celebrated their love with a spring wedding, the air sweet with the scent of blossoms. Life had more sweetness in store - just three months later, we welcomed our first grandchild, Karen Marie. She was such a precious gift, arriving with angelic wisps of blonde ringlets just like her mother before her. I remember holding her for the first time, those big turquoise eyes sparkling up at me like freshly polished beach glass. "She's perfect," I whispered, "absolutely perfect."

But as often happens in life, things changed after her marriage to Christopher. His interests lay more with cars and racing with his friends, and gradually, like a slowly fading song, Raelene stopped attending band practices and performances. "Sometimes life takes you in different directions," she'd say quietly whenever anyone asked about her pipes. Watching that part of her slip away was difficult for all of us who had seen how much joy it brought her.

Raelene and Christopher's joy doubled on October 15th, 1970, when their son Darryl Scott joined the family. Unlike his sister's curly locks, Scott came into the world with straight, buttery flaxen hair, though he shared the same cherubic features that seemed to run in our family. The following March, in 1971, they put down roots in Ingle Farm, purchasing their first home - a cosy Housing Trust dwelling that they gradually made their own.

But not all fairy tales end happily ever after. By 1984, Raelene and Christopher's marriage had run its course. Sometimes life has other plans, and in this case, those plans involved a connection from her past - Chris Scott, the son of her old Levi's coworker Margaret. *Life's funny sometimes, how everything comes full circle.* By September 1985, Raelene and Chris were engaged, ready to write a new chapter together.

That chapter began with a bold move to Darwin, where Chris worked for AGC Business Finance while Raelene found her place at Westpac. It was during their time up north that Raelene experienced the joy of becoming a grandmother herself - Karen gave birth to a beautiful baby girl named Crystal on December 8, 1986. "Now you know exactly how I felt," I told her as she cradled her granddaughter, tears of joy in her eyes.

July 1988 saw them packing up their Darwin life and heading to Sydney, where they bought a unit in Carlingford. The aroma of their Chinese neighbours' cooking became a constant companion, filling the air with exotic spices. But the biggest surprise was yet to come - on December 21, 1990, Raelene and Chris tied the knot in a private ceremony, keeping it secret until Christmas when they delighted everyone with their wedding photos. "Surprise!" they announced, passing around their album during Christmas dinner. What a gift that was!

Their Sydney story continued in September 1992 with a move to a lovely house in Cherrybrook. But Adelaide's pull proved strong, and by August 1996, they were ready to return home. "There's just something about Adelaide," Raelene admitted. "It keeps calling you back." She secured a promotion at the Mortgage Loan Centre in Lockleys, while Chris stayed behind temporarily to sell their Sydney home before joining her at the same workplace.

In October 1997, they achieved another milestone - building their dream home in Grange. Meanwhile, their family continued to grow as Karen, now married to Damien McCall, blessed them with two more grandchildren.

Raelene never lost her capacity to surprise us. Years later, when she turned fifty in September 1999, she shocked everyone - especially her daughter Karen - by revealing her first and only tattoo. "Well, what do you think?" she asked with that familiar twinkle in her eye. It was such a perfect expression of how she'd always lived life: doing things her own way, in her own time, yet never afraid to embrace something new.

Through all these changes - the moves from Darwin to Sydney and back to Adelaide, the career shifts, the growing family - Raelene and Chris built something beautiful together. Their journey wasn't always straightforward, but then again, the best stories rarely are. Now that I think about it, it's clear that each step, each decision, led them exactly where they were meant to be.

Life has a way of testing our strength, and Raelene faced her share of health challenges along the way. During her time at Levi's, she began experiencing trouble with her ear. The doctors recommended a complicated procedure called a Stapedectomy - just saying the word was difficult enough, let alone going through the operation itself. "Well," she said with characteristic determination, "we'll just have to get on with it, won't we?" But Raelene faced it with the quiet courage she'd always shown. As if one wasn't enough, ten years later her other ear required the same procedure. Like so many things in her life, she handled it with grace, adapting to each challenge as it came.

The joy of being a grandmother seemed to make any hardship worthwhile. I still remember the pride in Raelene's eyes when Karen's first child, Crystal, was born on December 8, 1986, while Raelene and Chris were living in Darwin. "Mum," she called me that evening, her voice soft with wonder, "Now I understand how you felt when you first held Karen." Despite the distance, that bond between grandmother and granddaughter grew strong from the very beginning.

Karen's marriage to Damien McCall brought more blessings to our expanding family. Christopher Shane arrived on June 4, 1991, a bouncing baby boy who shared his grandmother's bright spirit. Not long after, on November 6, 1992, Dylan Ray joined the family, completing Karen and Damien's trio of children. *Three grandchildren,* Raelene would muse, *how rich life can be.*

Watching Raelene with her grandchildren reminded me so much of her own early days of motherhood. The same gentle touch, the same patient smile, the same unconditional love - just as she had shown with Karen and Scott. Her grandchildren brought out a special light in her, a joy that seemed to make her glow from within. "There's nothing quite like it," she told me once, "seeing your own children's children grow."

The years have brought many changes to our family - marriages, moves, careers, and challenges. Through it all, Raelene has remained that same spirited girl who once surprised us by wanting to learn the bagpipes, who raced off to see The Beatles, and who made her own path in life. From that tiny baby born with a caul in 1949 to the grandmother who got her first tattoo at fifty, she's always done things her own way. "Life's too short for regrets," she often says, and she's lived by those words.

I now realise that, looking at her today, surrounded by her family in that beautiful Grange home she built with Chris, I see the same bright spirit that's always been there - just a bit wiser, a bit more seasoned by life's ups and downs. Each chapter of her life - daughter, wife, mother, grandmother - has added new depths to her story, and I count myself blessed to have witnessed it all.

What does it feel like to lose a child before they're born? How does a mother's heart heal from such a deep wound? These are questions I faced during a particularly difficult time in our family's story. After Raelene, I had Bryce, whose story you'll read in the next chapter. Between Bryce and Lesley, life gave us both sorrow and joy, teaching us just how precious each child truly is.

I was very sick for five and a half months with that pregnancy, in and out of the hospital more times than I care to remember. Then one evening, when I finally felt well enough, our neighbours invited us to a party. The music and laughter seemed like such a welcome change after all those months of illness. I even felt strong enough to dance that night. But the next day, we lost our little boy. Back then, there were no funerals for babies lost this way, no ceremonies to mark their passing. It was a quiet kind of heartbreak that mothers carried alone.

Perhaps that's why Lesley's arrival felt like such a precious gift. We call her Lel now - a nickname that stuck because that's how her brothers and sisters pronounced her name when they were little. "Lel! Lel!" they'd call, their voices full of love for their baby sister.

She came into our world on Tuesday, November 27th, 1953, at the Onkaparinga District Hospital in Woodside. We were living there while Ron was in the Army, and I remember thinking what a tiny thing she was, barely six pounds. But oh, what a perfect six pounds! After our previous loss, each ounce felt like a miracle.

Lel was such a content baby, peaceful in a way that seemed to come naturally to her. Maybe it was because we already had a houseful of children and were always busy, or maybe she just had that calm soul from the start. When she did want attention, though, it was like a race between her siblings - each one wanting to be the first to pick her up before we could even get there! "My turn, my turn!" they'd shout, eager to hold their precious baby sister.

But life has its ways of testing us, and our little Lel faced her first big challenge when she was about eighteen months old. We moved to Sandilands after Ron left the Army and started working for Len Gersch. Before that, he'd spent some time working on the roads - you know how it is when you're trying to make ends meet. With all the moving and new jobs, somehow Lel's immunisations got overlooked. I wish we'd been more careful about that.

It started as just a cold, nothing to worry about, really. But then came that terrible cough. Have you ever heard a child with whooping cough? It's a sound that haunts you - like a seal barking, they say, but so much worse when it's your own child struggling to breathe. Poor Lel was sick for months, losing weight until she was just a shadow of herself. We took turns sitting up with her night after day after night, doing everything we could to help her through each coughing spell. She did get better, thank heavens, but stayed thin as a reed for the longest time afterwards.

School brought its own challenges as we moved from place to place. Her first school was in Whyte Yarcowie, just a tiny country school where everyone knew everyone else. Later, she went to school in Geranium when we lived in Parrakie - old enough by then to help with milking the cows! Each move meant a new school, new friends to make, but Lel took it all in stride. By the time we settled in Edwardstown, she'd learned to adapt quickly, making friends with Jane Keeler (now Jane McKellar) and Jan Stasinowski almost right away.

Around eight years old, Lel found her passion in netball. "Mum," she'd say, her eyes shining, "did you see that goal?" She played for years, right into adulthood, until problems with her knee led to an operation and forced her to give up the game she loved. But that was Lel - when one door closed, she'd simply look for another to open.

Through all these early years - the moves, the illness, the schools, the sports - Lel showed us a quiet strength that would define her character. Each challenge seemed to add another layer to who she was becoming, like pages in a book slowly revealing its story.

❖

Lel's journey into adulthood began at the Bank of New South Wales (now called Westpac). I can still picture her in her crisp bank uniform, looking so grown up it almost took my breath away. But life had bigger plans for my quiet, strong girl, and they arrived in the form of a young man named Trevor Porter - though everyone called him Tich.

They met at her friend Jan Stasinowski's house one February evening in 1971. You know how sometimes you can just tell when something special is happening? It was like watching two puzzle pieces find each other. Their love story unfolded quickly, as young love often does, and before we knew it, they were planning a wedding.

October 16, 1971, dawned bright and full of promise. Lel chose a beautiful pant suit instead of a traditional dress - that was just like her, practical yet perfect. As I watched her that day, my mind flashed back to that tiny six-pound baby we brought home from Onkaparinga District Hospital. Now here she was, starting her own story.

The newlyweds set up their first home in a small flat in Kurralta Park. It wasn't much, but they filled it with love and dreams. Lel had started working at Hubbard's Department Store by then, in stock control. She had always been good with details and numbers - a trait that would serve her well as she built her life with Tich.

In 1985, when jobs were scarce as desert rain, Tich found work in Gove, Northern Territory. For seven years, he worked from home - our little piece of the Territory right here in South Australia. Then, like birds testing their wings, Lel and Tich took flight to Hong Kong in 1988, beginning their love affair with travel.

In 1991, our family circle widened when we welcomed Yoko, an exchange student from Japan. She brought such sweetness into our home, like sunshine through a window. That same year, though, brought an even bigger joy - we became grandparents when Kymberly gave birth to Breeanna Carol-Ann on December 15th at Flinders Medical Centre. Have you ever seen a new grandmother's smile? It's like holding sunshine in your heart.

Life had more changes in store. March 1992 saw Tich start work at W.M.C. in Roxby Downs, and by April 16th, Lel, Kym, and little Breeanna had joined him there. Watching them pack up and move north was like watching a chapter close and another begin.

In Roxby Downs, Lel found her calling working with children. From 1993 to 1996, she studied at T.A.F.E. while working at the Child Care Centre, and later moved to the Roxby Downs Kindergarten. Her days filled with children's laughter and tiny discoveries. Our family web kept growing when we hosted another exchange student, Reiko, in 1997. Meanwhile, Shane's life took him first to Melbourne, then to Sydney, like a leaf carried on life's breeze.

1999 brought more surprises - Kymberly, Jamey, and Breeanna eloped! Then came another precious gift: grandson Ethan Hugh, born on November 14th. The next year, Lel and Breeanna embarked on their own adventure to Japan, visiting both Reiko and Yoko. How strange and wonderful to see our family connections spanning oceans!

Life isn't always gentle, though, is it? In January 2000, Tich had a terrible fall from a ladder, injuring his back. Those two weeks he spent in Adelaide Hospital felt like two years. But just as our family had weathered every storm before, we weathered this one, too. Tich recovered, though his back still troubles him sometimes.

Sometimes love shows itself in the simplest ways, doesn't it? Like when Lel and Tich gave me their old computer. Or when Tich built me this perfect desk where I sit writing our family's story. These aren't just gifts - they're pieces of their hearts, given freely.

As I sit at my desk that Tich made just for me, writing these stories on the computer they so kindly gave me, I feel a warm glow inside. Sometimes I wonder what I'll do when I finish writing about our family - it's become such a big part of my life. But looking back at Lel's journey, from that tiny six-pound baby to the grandmother she is today, I can't help but feel blessed. The quiet strength she showed as a child has only grown stronger with time. Through every move, every challenge, every joy, she's faced life with that same gentle determination. Perhaps that's the greatest gift parents can receive - watching our children grow into people who make us proud in ways we never imagined.

CHAPTER 12

From Storms To Sanctuary

The Queen Victoria Maternity Hospital buzzed with its usual activity that April morning in 1951, but for me, everything felt different. My face was swollen beyond recognition, and the doctors kept me isolated, puzzled by my condition. Through the fog of my own medical challenges, I welcomed my son Bryce Allen Clark into the world - a robust eight-pound baby named after Ron's old school friend. Even in those first difficult days, when I could barely leave my bed, I sensed this child would have a unique journey.

Those early years on the farm seemed idyllic at first. Bryce was an active little boy, full of curiosity about the world around him. Not all farm memories were peaceful ones, though. When Bryce was just three, his fascination with matches led to a heart-stopping moment during harvest season.

I was inside when I heard the commotion - Ron had spotted smoke from the paddock and came running. The verandah posts were catching fire, and our four girls were in the bath when Ron burst in, grabbing hessian bags to wet them. I can still picture him running in and out through the window, red-faced and determined, while the girls huddled at one end of the tub. We managed to put the fire out, and Bryce got a stern lesson about playing with matches that day.

Years later, Bryce captured this memory in a poem that showed both his creative spirit and his ability to see humour in even serious moments:

My father and fire

Funny things occur with little sisters in the Bath
And Dad comes running in and out-- a flaming fire on his path.

Just a little match and box;
My play and flamin' hell, the - grass.

In and out the window.
He yells, "Wet the bags and throw 'em on;
Douse those flames, verandah's nearly gone".
And there I am, I'm thinking, "Just a little match"

Now the bath is getting low.
My sisters, their all dry and huddled up at the end.
Dad is red and flyin' in again.

I'll survive, I know,
With memories etched upon my tail;
The girls and hessian bags and bath.
My flyin' Father, red with fire on the path.
And then there's me, and just a little match
And box and flamin' hell the grass.

Reading his words now, I can see how even this frightening incident held the seeds of who Bryce would become - someone who could transform difficult experiences into insights that would help others. Though I must admit, his fascination with fire didn't end there - there would be another incident in grade seven that had us all holding our breath again.

I remember clearly the day in December 1953 when my heart swelled with pride as my four-year-old stood in the Parrakie Methodist Church, confidently reciting John 3:16 at the Sunday School end-of-year celebration. He won a prize that day, but more than that, he showed the first glimpses of the spiritual connection that would later shape his life.

But motherhood rarely follows a straight path, and our journey with Bryce had its share of curves and detours. When he was just eight months old, our living situation became challenging. The caravan at Woodside was simply too small for a growing, active baby. Our friends, Pat and Beth Feehan, offered to care for him temporarily - a decision that, while necessary, weighed heavily on my heart. For two months, I missed his daily presence, even as I knew he was surrounded by love and attention.

As I think on this, I wonder if these early separations left their mark. The most difficult came during our family holiday to Pt. Victoria. We left Bryce at Kate Cocks Babies Home in Hove, following the professional advice of the time. They didn't believe in dummies there, and though I'd mentioned Bryce could drink from a cup, I'd forgotten to tell them he still needed his bottle. My heart aches now, thinking of my little one, separated from his family and his familiar comforts all at once.

When we returned, we discovered Bryce had developed a troubling habit - banging his head against his cot. It was as if he were speaking a language of loss we didn't yet understand. This behaviour continued for what seemed like ages, each thump against the rails echoing the gaps in our understanding of what our little boy needed.

The move to the city in 1960 marked another seismic shift in our lives. Gone were the wide-open spaces of farm life, replaced by the cramped quarters of my mother's two-bedroom house. Bryce and his brother slept on the front verandah, while his four sisters shared the second bedroom. I watched my nine-year-old son struggle to adjust, his confidence seeming to shrink in the urban environment.

The physical challenges came next. At ten, Bryce spent

several weeks in the hospital, followed by more weeks in a back and leg splint. I saw his social connections, already fragile from the move, begin to unravel. The little boy who once recited Scripture with such confidence seemed to retreat into himself.

Yet even in these challenging times, grace found its way to us. The Edwardstown Baptist Church became Bryce's sanctuary, a place where he felt accepted and valued. At eleven, during a Christian Endeavour camp in the Adelaide Hills, he had a profound spiritual experience, giving his heart to Jesus. Watching Reverend Colin Asser baptise my son shortly after, I felt a mixture of joy and hope - hope that perhaps this spiritual foundation would help anchor him through whatever storms lay ahead.

These early years taught me that motherhood requires equal measures of love and faith. As I watched Bryce navigate his challenges - the head-banging, the difficult transitions, the physical ailments - I learned to trust both my maternal instincts and God's greater plan. Each stage brought its own lessons, its own fears, and its own small victories.

What I didn't know then was that these early chapters were just the beginning of a much longer story - one that would test our family's strength, challenge our faith, and ultimately reveal the extraordinary resilience of a boy who would grow up to help others find their way through their own dark times.

How does a mother's heart prepare for storms she cannot see coming?

The call from the Brighton Police station that day felt like a lightning bolt through my ordinary afternoon at work. Bryce, my fifteen-year-old son, had been caught drunk on the jetty. As I rushed to collect him, my mind raced with questions I couldn't answer. *Where had my little boy gone - the one who once recited Bible verses with such innocent joy?*

When I saw him at the station, head bowed and fighting tears, maternal instinct took over. "Lift your head up," I told him firmly, "you're my son and be proud of it." But later that night, alone in my room, I whispered prayers into my pillow. *Lord, show us the way through this. Give us the strength we need.*

The incident became our turning point. When the Service to Youth Council became involved, I had such high hopes. *Finally,* I thought, *we'll get the help we need.* But watching them send a young woman to counsel Bryce while Ron and I spoke with a man, I couldn't shake the feeling that something wasn't quite right.

Then came the call that changed everything - the psychiatrist warning us that Bryce wanted to run away to the bush. *The only thing stopping him,* he said, *was how much he loved his family.* Those words still resound in my mind, a bittersweet testament to the bonds that both bound and saved us.

Nothing could have prepared me for that day at Glenside. Walking away from that small room with its soft walls and barred windows, leaving my fifteen-year-old behind - it felt like my heart was being torn from my chest. Ron and I cried all day. *Even now, decades later, the memory brings tears to my eyes.*

But Bryce surprised us all during those eight weeks. The staff said he had a calming effect on other patients. I remember visiting him and watching him quietly ask a boy to turn down his blaring radio - and the boy actually did it with a smile. *My son, even in his own darkness, was finding ways to help others see light.*

The diagnosis - Schizophrenia - felt like both a relief and a sentence. Finally, we had a name for our struggles, but with it came the heavy weight of "always." The doctors said he would need medication forever. *Forever is such a long time when you're watching your child suffer.*

We tried a new approach at home. When Bryce had his outbursts, instead of punishment, we gave him extra love. It wasn't easy - especially trying to balance this with fairness to his siblings. *Sometimes love looks like inconsistency to those who don't understand the deeper need.*

The years that followed brought their own challenges. Watching Bryce struggle with a back injury, then survive heartbreak when his first serious relationship ended - each trial felt like another test of our family's resilience. His father and I worried constantly, but we tried to keep faith.

Then, at twenty-three, Bryce made an announcement that terrified me: he wanted to stop his medication. "If God wants me to be sick, I will be," he declared. "If he wants me to be better, I will be." *Oh, how those words scared me! But sometimes a mother's greatest act of love is trusting her child's journey with God.*

And then, the miracle we hadn't dared to hope for - Bryce got better. The son who had once been confined to a room with barred windows was walking freely in the world again. *Had our prayers been answered, or had this been God's plan all along?*

In retrospect, I see how each crisis shaped not just Bryce, but all of us. His siblings learned compassion in ways few children do. Ron and I discovered strengths we never knew we had. And Bryce? Well, Bryce learned that love doesn't give up, even when the storms seem endless.

Sometimes I look at him now and remember that little boy on the Brighton Jetty, head bowed in shame. Then I see the man he's become – strong, compassionate, healed – and I understand that every storm, no matter how fierce, carries the seeds of transformation within it.

After watching my son weather so many storms, seeing him find love felt like witnessing a miracle in bloom. *How strange, I thought, that heartbreak could lead to such joy.* It started with a simple visit – Bryce riding his little Honda 50 to see a friend of his former girlfriend. But God had other plans that day, and her name was Judy.

I'll never forget watching them together during their courtship. They approached their relationship with such intentional faith – praying together, studying Scripture, and discovering their shared calling. When they decided to marry after just six months of knowing each other, some people thought it was too quick. But I saw something different: I saw two souls who recognised God's hand in their meeting.

Their wedding in January 1975 at the Edwardstown Baptist

Church felt like a fresh chapter opening. Bryce was 24, Judy was 22, and their faces shone with hope. Standing in that church, watching my son speak his vows, I remembered all the prayers I'd whispered during those dark nights at Glenside. *Lord, you were listening all along, weren't you?*

The years that followed brought more blessings than I could have imagined. First came Teena Joy in 1976, then Tracey Lee in 1977, and Sonya Michelle in 1979. Each granddaughter felt like another flower blooming in our family garden. When they later opened their hearts to foster daughter Naomi Steele, I saw in Bryce and Judy the same unconditional love we had tried to show him during his difficult years.

But Bryce wasn't content to simply build a family - he felt called to something more. While Judy worked full-time to support them, he began his studies at the New Creation Church in Coromandel Valley. I watched with pride as he pursued his education with the same determination he'd once shown in fighting his illness. From Bible College to Lutheran Seminary, each achievement felt like another victory over those dark predictions from his youth.

Who would have thought, I often wondered, *that the boy who once needed so much help would become someone who helps others?* Yet there he was, earning his Master of Religious Studies, transforming his past struggles into a wellspring of compassion for others.

In November 1999, when Bryce became a Lutheran Minister at Ferryden Park, my heart nearly burst with pride. The congregation there is beautifully diverse - Aboriginal people, Asian families, African immigrants - all finding comfort in my son's guidance. Every time Ron and I visit his church, we're touched by the warm welcome we receive. *This,* I think, *is what healing looks like when it comes full circle.*

His ministry is special because he understands struggle from the inside out. When he counsels someone facing mental health challenges or family difficulties, he speaks not just from theological training but from lived experience. The boy who once felt lost now helps others find their way.

Sometimes, when we're all together - our growing family with all its branches and blossoms - I catch myself marvelling at how far we've come. We still have our family joke: whenever something goes wrong, we say, "Bryce did it!" And now he laughs along with us, secure in who he is and in God's love for him.

Looking at Bryce now - respected minister, loving husband, devoted father and grandfather - I see more than just my son. I see a testament to faith, to family love, to the power of never giving up. His journey from patient to pastor reminds me that God's plans are bigger than our fears, and His grace is more powerful than any diagnosis.

Perhaps, I think sometimes, *this was God's plan all along - not to prevent the storms, but to use them to shape a heart that could help others through their own dark weather.* In Bryce's story, I see echoes of every parent's hopes, fears, and dreams, and the reminder that love, in all its forms, is the most powerful medicine of all.

As I reflect on the decades of Bryce's journey, I'm struck by life's mysterious ways. *Who would have imagined that the confused young boy in Glenside would one day counsel others through their own valleys of darkness?* The transformation from patient to pastor wasn't just a career change - it was proof of God's healing power and the strength of the human spirit.

In his ministry work, Bryce brings something special to those struggling with mental health. When he sits with troubled souls in his office at Ferryden Park, there's no textbook sympathy in his words. Instead, there's the deep understanding of someone who has walked through the fire and emerged stronger. *Sometimes,* he once told me, *the greatest ministry happens when we simply sit with people in their pain, because we remember what it felt like to sit there ourselves.*

Our family has grown and healed alongside Bryce. The grandchildren - Luan Thomas, Aldan James, Kelsie Grace, Jami Jayde, and Keiran John - bring such joy to our gatherings. When I watch Bryce with them, telling stories or offering gentle guidance, I see no trace of the troubled teenager who once banged his head against his cot. Instead, I see a grandfather who has learned to turn his scars into lessons of love and resilience.

We've learned to find humour in our journey, too. That old family joke - "Bryce did it!" - has become more than just a saying. It's our way of acknowledging that while the past held its struggles, we're strong enough now to laugh about them. Bryce joins in the laughter, secure in the knowledge that he's so much more than his past challenges.

The medical world played its part in Bryce's recovery, yes. But it was faith that gave us the strength to keep going when the doctors' predictions seemed dire. It was family love that held us together through the darkest nights. And it was community - from those early days at Edwardstown Baptist Church to his current Lutheran congregation - that showed us we were never alone.

Sometimes I sit in his church, watching him guide his diverse congregation with such gentle wisdom, and I remember that day at the Brighton Police Station. "Lift your head up," I told him then. "You're my son, and be proud of it." Today, he lifts others' heads, helping them find pride and purpose in their own journeys.

This story - our story - isn't just about mental health or religious faith or family bonds. It's about how all these knit together to create something stronger than any single strand could be alone. It's about how God can use our deepest wounds to help heal others, and how love can transform even our darkest chapters into sources of light.

When people ask me about Bryce's journey now, I tell them this: sometimes the path to healing isn't about leaving our struggles behind, but about learning to use them to light the way for others. My son, who once needed so much help, now helps others find their way home to themselves.

And isn't that the greatest miracle of all?

The little boy who lost his dummy at Kate Cocks Babies

Home, who struggled through adolescence, who fought against mental illness - he didn't just survive. He thrived. And in thriving, he learned to help others do the same.

Our family's story continues to unfold, each new chapter bringing its own challenges and joys. But now we face them together, stronger for having weathered past storms, wiser for having learned that love and faith can carry us through anything.

And sometimes, when we're all together - children, grandchildren, extended family - I catch Bryce's eye across the room and see in his smile the truth we've learned: that every broken piece, when held in God's hands, can become part of something beautiful.

That's the legacy I hope our story leaves: that no matter how *dark the night, dawn always comes. And sometimes, just sometimes, the deepest wounds become the greatest gifts we have to offer the world.*

CHAPTER 13

Roots and Wings: The Story of Glenda Clark

They say babies choose their own timing, but Glenda Jean Clark had a flair for the dramatic from the start. Not only did she pick a stormy night to begin her journey, but she also decided to enter the world bottom-first, as if doing a somersault onto life's stage. It was September 1956, and while the wind howled and rain battered the windows of Jamestown Hospital, our little acrobat was taking her sweet time, waiting until the next day to make her grand entrance.

You know how they say every baby has their own personality right from the start? Well, Glenda proved that true from her very first moment. Most babies come out headfirst, but not our

Glenda! She decided to come out bottom first, with her tiny feet tucked under her chin, like she was doing a somersault into life.

"She's breech," I heard Dr Bentley announce.

"Bottom first, with her feet tucked under her chin. I guess you're roomy inside, so she got plenty of space for her acrobatics "When I think about it, I agree it was a sign of how she'd approach life - always finding her own unique way.

What makes a mother's heart sing with joy? Is it the first cry of a newborn, or the small victories that follow? After Glenda was born, something wonderful happened. I got to walk back to my room - something unheard of in those days when mothers were kept in bed for days after having a baby. It felt like a small taste of freedom, holding my new little one close as I stretched my legs.

Have you ever watched how a family grows and changes with each new addition? Our home was already bustling with four older children, but Glenda brought her own special magic. The best part was seeing how much the older kids loved her. There was no jealousy, just pure excitement. Everyone wanted their turn to hold the baby, like a precious gift they all shared. Feeding time became like a game of musical chairs, with each child eagerly waiting for their chance to cuddle Glenda.

What makes a house on a farm become a home? How do children's laughter and daily chores create childhood memories? In Dillowie, our days had a rhythm all their own. Between collecting eggs, gathering wood for fires, and taking care of everyone, there was always something to do. The children grew close in those wide-open spaces, sharing work and play under the big country sky.

But life, like the seasons, brings change. When Glenda was about two years old, our family packed up and moved to Parrakie. We lived and worked on Ernie Hubble's property for about two years, adding new chapters to our family story.

When the time came to move to town, we settled into Nana Clark's house in Edwardstown. How different it was from our farm life! Instead of open fields, we had neighbours close by. The sounds of livestock were replaced by city noises, and our wide horizons became street views and garden fences.

This was where Glenda started school for the first time. Can you imagine what it's like for a farm child to step into a town school? Our house became a hub of education - three children at Edwardstown Primary School and two at Marion High School. It was like running our own little school sometimes!

Through all these changes, one thing about Glenda tugged at my heartstrings. She was our homebody, our nest-keeper. Even when she was older and would stay at a friend's house, we'd often get those late-night calls. She'd be crying, wanting to come home. It was hard to see her struggle, but we always went to pick her up. Sometimes I wonder if those early years on the farm had planted such deep roots in her heart that any other place felt strange and unfamiliar.

"Mum, I want to come home." Those late-night calls became a familiar tune in our house. No matter whose sleepover it was or how much fun was promised, Glenda's homesickness would creep in like evening shadows. "It's okay, love," I'd say, climbing into the car yet again. "Home's not going anywhere."

Every summer brought a new challenge - the government swimming classes at the beach. "I just can't do it, Mum," Glenda would say, her voice trembling as much as her body in the cold water. But she kept trying. Four years it took her to get that beginner's certificate, dog-paddling her way through. Even now, she laughs and says, "I still can't really swim!"

The same determination showed up when she decided to get her driver's license at eighteen. Three tries it took, but that third time, her face beamed with pride as she waved that license in the air. "See, Mum? I did it!"

What makes a young heart ready to try new things? How does independence grow, even in someone who loves home so deeply?

✿

Glenda's first step into the working world was at Thredgold's Pharmacy in Edwardstown. "Good morning, can I help you?" - I can still hear her practising those words at home. After that came Bryson Jaguar cars in Adelaide, and then W.A. Young Shadehouses. Each job was like a small step away from the nest.

At seventeen, love knocked on her door. "His name is Andrew Simonds, Mum," she told me, eyes sparkling. They got engaged, and for four and a half years, it seemed like her future was set.

But life had other plans. When they broke up, I held her while she cried for days. "Will it always hurt this much?" she asked. These are the moments when a mother's heart breaks, too.

But sometimes, life's biggest surprises come when we least expect them. In 1980, Honda gave us a wonderful opportunity - a trip to Japan! "You're coming too," I told Glenda. She looked uncertain at first, but oh, how that trip changed her!

"Look at all these buildings, Mum!" she'd exclaim, her eyes wide with wonder. It was like watching a flower slowly unfold its petals. Each day in Japan, she grew a little more confident, a little more adventurous.

That taste of the world seemed to awaken something in her. Back home, she worked her way up at different places - Ford Electrical, Myers in Adelaide, and then Tupperware in Edwardstown. "I'm going to be a manager," she announced one day, and before we knew it, she had her own station wagon with the company name on it!

But the biggest surprise came in 1981. "I'm moving to Alice Springs," she declared one day. My heart skipped a beat - our homebody was heading to the heart of Australia! She got a job at Murray Neck Retravision, and off she went.

Six months later, though, she was back home. "It was too far, Mum," she said simply. That same pull that had brought her home from childhood sleepovers had reached across the desert to bring her back. But something was different now - she'd tried it, she'd spread her wings, and even though she chose to return, she knew she could fly if she wanted to.

I have come to realise how each step - even the ones that led back home - helped shape who Glenda would become. Those tears at sleepovers, the determination at swimming lessons, the heartbreak with Andrew, the excitement in Japan, the adventure in Alice Springs - they were all part of her journey.

"You know, Mum," she told me recently, "sometimes you have to go away to really understand where you belong." And isn't that the truth of it? Sometimes the heart's pull toward home is just as important as the courage to spread your wings.

I often sit here in my kitchen, looking out at the garden, and think about how our children grow in such different ways. Have you ever felt that invisible string that ties you to home? For Glenda, that pull was strong from her earliest days. Sometimes I wonder if it started during that stormy night before she was born, when the wind howled like it was trying to keep her close to me.

Even as a young girl, spending nights away from home was like trying to stretch an elastic band too far - it always snapped back. I can still hear those late-night phone calls clear as day, her voice wobbling on the other end of the line, asking to come home from sleepovers at friends' houses. We never minded picking her up; it was just part of who she was, like her playful smile or the way she could brighten a room. Lord knows I've driven those dark streets enough times, my heart aching for my homesick girl.

Those calls didn't mean she was weak - far from it. Our Glenda had a quiet determination that showed itself in the most surprising ways. Take those government swimming classes at the beach every Christmas holiday. Most children would zip through their beginner's certificate in a season or two, but Glenda took her own path. Four years of dog paddling, never giving up despite the salt water in her eyes and the endless practices. I can still see her now, paddling away with such concentration, never minding the other children swimming past her with their perfect strokes.

That same persistence showed up years later when she tackled getting her driver's license. Three attempts it took her, each try teaching her something new. I used to joke that it took her four tries to learn to swim but only three to learn to drive - that always made her laugh. Sitting here now, I realise how those small struggles shaped her character, like water slowly smoothing a stone.

From that stormy night when she entered the world feet first (always doing things her own way!), to the confident woman she became, Glenda's story reminds us that life isn't about how far you go, but about knowing where you belong. And sometimes, like in Glenda's case, the greatest achievement is having the courage to be exactly who you are. Looking at her now, helping me with my shopping and keeping me company, I see all those versions of my daughter at once - the homesick little girl, the determined swimmer, the adventurous traveller

- and my heart swells with pride.

Sitting here with my photo albums spread across the kitchen table, touching the faces frozen in time, I remember it all so clearly. In March 1984, love opened a new chapter in Glenda's story when she married Neil Treuel. The day they left by train for Darwin, where Neil hoped to find work as a mechanic, I watched tears roll down Glenda's cheeks. My own heart was so full - happy for her new adventure but aching at the thought of the distance between us. Even in her happiness, that familiar tug of home pulled at her heart. Sometimes I wonder if she knew then that she was already carrying a precious secret - they didn't know yet, but a new life was growing inside her.

Have you ever experienced joy so pure it makes your heart overflow? That's how I felt when I held my granddaughter Julie for the first time. Born on January 22, 1985, she came into the world with the most beautiful red hair you've ever seen. Lord, how that red hair reminded me of my own mother! Ron and I were in Alice Springs when we heard the news, and we took the first bus we could to Darwin. I remember walking into their small flat, the January heat pressing down like a heavy blanket. Even now, I can feel that oppressive Darwin heat, see the worry on my daughter's tired face as she tried to soothe her newborn in that stifling flat with no air conditioning.

When I reached out to hold Julie, Neil said, "She won't come to you." But like a magnet to metal, she came right into my arms. I knew she would - there's a special bond between grand-mothers and their grandbabies that can't be explained. I still smile remembering Neil's surprised face. Sometimes I think about that moment when I'm holding my other grandchildren, that instant connection that spans generations.

Life is like a garden, though, with both blooming flowers and wilting leaves. In 1986, a shadow fell over our family when Glenda and Neil's baby boy, Jamie, was stillborn. Oh, how do you find words for such moments? We laid him to rest at Centennial Park Cemetery, our hearts heavy with dreams that would never be. It was like a little star that never got to shine, but its memory still twinkles in our hearts. Even now, decades later, my throat tightens when I pass that cemetery.

But just as spring follows winter, joy returned to us. On February 25, 1987, Kerry Joanne burst into the world at Flinders Medical Centre, bringing her own special light. Not a redhead like her sister, but just as precious. Sometimes when I watch Kerry now, I marvel at how different siblings can be. She grew into quite the character - more of a tomboy than a little lady, even playing football with the boys' team! I remember standing on the sidelines, watching her tackle those boys, thinking how life surprises you with its twists and turns.

Time has a way of changing things, doesn't it? In 1997, Glenda and Neil decided their paths needed to go in different directions. I worried at first - divorce is never easy on a family. But they showed us all how to handle it with grace. They divorced in 1998, but there was no bitterness or anger - just two people who still cared about each other and their girls. Watching them navigate this change with such maturity made me proud, though my heart ached for the dreams that wouldn't come true.

These days, Glenda has found companionship with John, a nice young man who brings his own kind of joy to her life. I watch them together sometimes, seeing how he makes her laugh, how good he is with Julie and Kerry. It reminds me that love has many chapters, and each one brings its own gifts.

Life has a funny way of bringing things full circle, doesn't it? Sometimes I sit at this very table, watching Glenda move around my kitchen, and I see echoes of myself at her age. Now she works as a care worker at Alabricare, looking after older people. I catch myself wondering if she remembers all the times I cared for her, now that she spends her days caring for others. There's something beautiful about that, isn't there?

She helps me with my vacuuming and takes me shopping when I need it. I don't need much help yet, thank goodness, and I hope it stays that way for a while. But there's comfort in knowing that the little girl I once cared for is now ready to care for me. Sometimes I see her watching me with that same worried look I used to give my own mother, and I have to hide my smile.

When I look at Glenda now, folding my laundry or organising my medications, I see all the chapters of her life at once - like transparent photographs layered over each other. The homesick little girl who needed to come home from sleepovers, the young woman who ventured all the way to Darwin, the mother who experienced both heartbreak and joy, and now the caring woman who brings comfort to others. It's like looking at a beautiful patchwork quilt, each square telling its own story but all of them stitched together with love.

Sitting here in my kitchen, looking out at the garden where Glenda and her siblings once played, I marvel at how life unfolds. That stormy night when she came into the world feet first seems both yesterday and a lifetime ago. Through all the changes - the moves, the marriages, the births, the losses - one thing has remained constant: the invisible thread that connects our hearts.

The little girl who once needed comfort has become the woman who gives comfort to others. The daughter who once called home in tears now makes her own home a place of warmth and welcome. And isn't that what life is really about? Not just growing up, but growing into the person you're meant to be, while keeping hold of the love that made you who you are. Looking at her now, I see all the best parts of our family's story continuing through her, and my heart swells with quiet pride.

CHAPTER 14

Ricky and Nown

Our family story holds a special chapter about a precious baby who was with us for just a brief moment in time. His name was Richard Kendrew Clark - Ricky to us - named after one of Ron's dear school friends. Even now, decades later, telling his story fills my heart with both joy and sadness.

Ricky came into our world on a Tuesday, May 10th, 1955, at Ardrossan Hospital. Dr Chard helped bring him into this world, and I can still remember the mix of anticipation and excitement that filled those hospital halls. Back then, we were living on the Gersch's farm in Sandilands, a simple life with Ted, Rae, and Bryce already keeping our home lively with their childhood energy.

Those precious months with Ricky were filled with tiny moments I hold dear. Every morning, he'd wake for his 6:00am feed, his little hand wrapping around my finger as he nursed. His face would light up when he saw us, and he'd wiggle with such joy it would make us all smile. The other children were fascinated by their baby brother - I remember how they'd gather around his cot, watching him with wonder and speaking in whispered voices so as not to startle him.

Just the day before everything changed, we'd taken Ricky for his regular checkup at the clinic. The doctor said he was doing well, and we had no reason to think otherwise. How could we know that would be our last visit?

That morning of August 29th, 1955, started like any other. Ted, Rae, and Bryce caught the bus to school, and I headed to the main house to get meat from Vera Gersch after Ricky's early morning feed. He went back to sleep so peacefully - he wasn't due for his next feed until ten. But when I returned to check on him, my world stopped turning. My beautiful baby boy, just three and a half months old, lay still in his cot, his face turned toward the mattress. In that moment, everything changed.

Vera G. acted quickly, calling the doctor while I stood there, unable to move, unable to believe what was happening. Because Ricky died at home, the police had to come too. Back then, they called it "Cot Death," though nowadays they say SIDS. The doctor assured the police that Ricky had been well cared for - she'd seen him herself just the day before.

What happened next feels like a blur tinged with surreal

details I'll never forget. The doctor had brought her three Pekinese dogs with her that day, so our precious Ricky, wrapped carefully in a hessian bag, had to be placed in the boot of her car. Even in our deepest grief, life had a way of throwing in these strange little moments that stick with you.

The funeral was small but filled with love. Auntie Viv brought Nana Hulbert from town, and the Gersches - Vera and Len - came with some friends from church. In the church foyer, a tiny white coffin stood open, holding our little angel. We laid him to rest in Ardrossan Cemetery, where a kind friend cemented the grave with a raised edge. Later, when we could afford it, we added marble chips to make it look nice.

Years later, the local Lions Club reached out with an offer to upgrade the graves and place a plaque on Ricky's resting place. We could choose the words ourselves. Though it was offered freely, we sent a donation, our hearts full of gratitude for their kindness.

Even now, whenever we travel to Roxby Downs, we make sure to visit Ricky's grave, laying flowers and spending quiet moments remembering. Bryce and Glenda make the journey too, keeping their brother's memory alive in their own way.

Sometimes I wonder what Ricky would have been like if he'd grown up. Would he have shared Ted's boisterous spirit or Rae's thoughtful nature? Or maybe he would have been entirely his own person. We'll never know, but that doesn't stop us from wondering, from remembering, from loving.

Ricky's life was brief - just three and a half months - but

the love we had for him, the love we still have, spans decades. Every visit to his grave, every retelling of his story, every quiet moment of remembrance keeps his memory alive in our hearts.

In the quiet moments when I visit his grave, watching the wind rustle through the trees, I feel close to him again. His story might bring tears to my eyes, but it also brings a smile to my heart, knowing that he was ours, even if just for a little while. Ricky will always be our baby, our angel, our cherished memory that we hold dear through all the years.

Life has a way of healing even the deepest wounds, though the scars remain part of who we are. Four years after losing Ricky, our family was blessed with another precious gift - our youngest child, Leonie Mavis Clark. We call her Nown, a name born from the sweet way her older brothers and sisters pronounced her name when they were little. Her story is one of new beginnings, of hope renewed, and of the way love continues to grow even after loss.

Nown's entry into the world was quite the adventure. It all began on a Sunday night in April 1959 when my water broke. The next morning, after getting the other children off to school, I called Lamaroo Hospital, seventeen miles away. Given my experience with previous births, they wanted me there straight away. But Nown, even then, had her own plans.

For two full days, we waited at the hospital. Dr Cock and

the nurses tried everything they knew to help things along, but Nown simply wasn't ready. By Wednesday, April 15th, everyone was exhausted - the medical staff, me, and probably Nown too. Just as they started discussing the possibility of a cesarean section, she finally decided it was time. When she arrived, we had a frightening moment discovering the cord was wrapped around her neck, but our little girl came through it all perfectly fine, as if she'd been protecting herself all along by waiting.

Those early days were filled with the bustle of her older siblings doting on their baby sister. They'd hover around her cot, each wanting their turn to hold her or make her smile. But when Nown was just six months old, our family faced another challenge. I needed an operation in Adelaide, and once again our community showed its heart. A kind housekeeper stepped in to help with the household, while Ron and the Troubridge family in Geranium took turns caring for Nown. Even as our youngest, she was already bringing people together.

Life took an unexpected turn when Nown was eighteen months old. Ernie Hubble decided to sell the farm where we lived in Sandilands, and suddenly our familiar world shifted. We packed up our rural life - the wide spaces, the farm animals, the endless sky - and moved to Nana Clark's house at No. 8 Leonard St. in Edwardstown. We purchased the house from the family after Nana's passing, but the transition from country to city life was a big adjustment for us all.

For little Nown, though, the move brought unexpected

blessings. Our new neighbour, Lee Puczkowski, became like a second mother to her when I started working at Tupperware. Lee had two boys, Jesse and Michael (Mikey), who quickly became Nown's playmates. The three of them would spend hours together, and Lee often said how much she enjoyed having a little girl around to balance out her house full of boys. Even after Nown started school, she'd spend her afternoons at Lee's until her older siblings came home. It was a special relationship that continued for years.

Nown's school days at Edwardstown Primary brought new adventures. Unlike her siblings, who had started their education in country schools, she began her schooling in the city. She adjusted well to city life, making friends easily and keeping up with her studies. By the time she reached Marion High School, she was fully settled into our suburban life.

During her time at Marion High, the school ran a special fundraiser that became part of our family's legacy there. They were building a new hall and asked families to "buy" a brick and have their names engraved on it. We contributed about $50 for our brick, never imagining that years later, even after the school was torn down for housing, that hall would still stand as a community centre. It's like a little piece of our family history, set in stone.

Those school years saw Nown growing into her own person. She was the last of our children to attend Marion High, and in many ways, her experience was different from her older siblings. While Ted, Rae, Bryce, and Glenda had memories of farm life to compare with city living, Nown's earliest memories were of our Edwardstown home, of playing with the Puczkowski boys, and of the busy streets of suburban life.

When Nown turned sixteen, she decided school wasn't for her anymore and stepped into the working world. Her first job was at a hosiery bar in Marion Shopping Centre - though that turned out to be quite a short chapter! The one-week trial lasted just three days. You could tell right away it wasn't the right fit for her, and even her boss could see it. Sometimes the wrong start leads us to the right places.

That's when I gave her what she calls a "gentle push" (though she says I made her do it!) toward applying at LeCornu Child Minding Centre. Looking after children in the ball pit might not sound like a career move, but those two years showed us glimpses of where her path might lead. Though Nown says now she didn't particularly enjoy it there, I remember differently - perhaps mothers see things children don't at the time.

After LeCornu's, Nown faced nine months without work, but she didn't stay idle. She volunteered her time looking after children in town, building experience that would serve her well later. Then, like an answer to prayers, the government started a program for people who had been out of work. At nineteen, Nown landed a six-month trial position at Flinders Medical Centre in Medical Records. Something clicked there - they saw what we'd always known about her capability and kept her on permanently.

❖

It was during these early working years, in 1979, that love found its way into Nown's life. Allen Liebelt came into the picture, and watching their relationship bloom was like seeing a garden come to life in spring. But their love faced an early test when we took Nown and Glenda on a Honda trip to Japan in November 1980.

That Japan trip was quite an adventure - though Nown might tell it differently! While Glenda embraced every moment of the experience, Nown's heart seemed to stay behind with Allen. Even with several young men on the trip who made good company, she missed Allen terribly. But you know what they say about absence making the heart grow fonder - when we returned home, their love had only grown stronger.

They got engaged in 1981, and on February 6, 1982, they married in a beautiful ceremony at the Edwardstown Baptist Church. It was a day filled with joy and promise. The very next day, Ron left for a Furniture Fair in Germany with William Haughton, and a week later, I joined him there for two weeks, exploring England and parts of Europe. It was like we were all starting new chapters - Nown and Allen in their married life, and us in our travels.

Their first home was a cosy unit in Bray Street, Plympton Park - just big enough for two young people starting out together. After about a year, they spread their wings and moved to a house on Larrimah Road, Morphett Vale. It cost them around $35,000 - a sum that seemed enormous at the time! They stayed there for about four years before life threw them a curveball. Money got tight, and they had to make the tough decision to sell and start renting.

Their next home was in Claret Street, where they spent four years making memories, followed by two years in a rental on Reynold Street, Morphett Vale. Finally, they found their permanent home on Wheatsheaf Road, Morphett Vale. Through all these moves, they kept building their life together, proving that home is more about who you're with than where you are.

The greatest joy came early one morning - 3:07 am to be exact - on February 22, 1985, when their first daughter, Danni Marie, was born at Flinders Medical Centre. Then, on Australia Day 1990, at 3:20 pm, Amy Jade joined the family, making it complete. Our family has always been blessed with beautiful babies, and these two girls were no exception.

After Amy's birth, Nown decided to take a break from her seventeen-year career at Flinders. For about two years, she stayed home and cared for other people's children alongside her own - a job that seemed to combine all her previous experience. Then in 1997, a new opportunity came along at the Doctor's Clinic in Morphett Vale. Her dedication and hard work there led to her promotion to Assistant Manager in March 2000.

Watching Nown grow from our youngest child into a capable professional and loving mother has been one of life's greatest joys. She's built a life filled with love, family, and achievement - finding her own way while keeping close to her roots. From that baby who took her time coming into the world, to the woman who's created such a wonderful life and family of her own, Nown has always done things in her own time and her own way.

CHAPTER 15

Between Two Houses

They say the hardest beginnings forge the strongest souls. Perhaps that's why my husband Ron's first breath in this world came as a whisper rather than a cry - a fragile start that would spark a chain of decisions no one could have predicted. Three weeks later, a grand motor car would pull away from a struggling farm, carrying a tiny infant toward a fate that would alter not just his life but the lives of thousands of others.

My husband, Ron, often tells me of his difficult entry into this world. His mother, Ada, already worn thin from farm life and previous births, struggled with the delivery. Ron himself, poor dear, came into the world with some health troubles of his own.

With Ada's health failing and the demands of farm life weighing heavily, the family had to make one of those heart-wrenching decisions that only a mother could understand. Ron's two maiden aunts, living in their grand house in Mount Gambier with their brother (the railway's main engine driver), stepped forward to take in this tiny three-week-old baby.

"We'll take good care of him," they promised Ada. Ron always pauses here when telling the story, his voice softening at the thought of his mother's sacrifice.

There's this photograph Ron showed me once, capturing his first remembered meeting with his mother. Such a precious moment, frozen in time. There he was, this tiny thing balanced on the running board of his aunt's impressive motor car.

"Look at those mudguards," he'd say every time, eyes twinkling with boyish excitement. "Just like those Formula 1 racing cars in the magazines!" Even then, his love for anything mechanical was showing through.

The education system back then was in quite a muddle, constantly changing the enrollment dates as Ron approached school age. He ended up starting school later than most children, but I've always thought those extra months in Mount Gambier were a blessing in disguise. Those aunts, with their grand house and motor car, gave him a gentle start in life after such a difficult beginning.

The Great Depression hit Ron's family particularly hard, especially after he lost his father in 1931. Legacy stepped in to help—though Ron once told me they almost missed helping his brother Laurie, who, at fourteen, was just barely young enough to qualify for their support.

"Every penny counted back then," Ron would say, shaking his head. "Poor Mum could barely stretch that soldier's pension to feed and educate us all."

Laurie, being the oldest, carried such a heavy burden on his young shoulders. "He was determined to get his leaving certificate," Ron would tell me proudly, describing how his brother would rush from secondary school classes straight to his job at that new factory in Edwardstown. But like so many young men of that generation, World War II interrupted those carefully laid plans.

The family's move to Edwardstown was a turning point - though not an easy one.

"It wasn't really a proper farm, you know," Ron would always insist when telling me about their country house. The authorities finally realised what his mother had known in her heart: it was too much for her to manage. Converting their government land settlement loan to a home loan for the Edwardstown property made practical sense, but the change was profound.

"Mum would just stand there sometimes," Ron once told me softly, "looking out the window at all those suburban streets. So different from the open country we'd left behind."

Ada faced it all with such quiet dignity - the loss of her husband, the struggles of the Depression, and this massive move to Edwardstown. Even now, I can see the deep admiration in

Ron's eyes when he speaks of his mother's strength during those years. "She never complained," he'd tell me, shaking his head in wonder. "Just kept putting one foot in front of the other for us kids."

The war's shadow stretched across the whole family, touching each of them in different ways. Laurie's determination to serve was pure Clark family spirit. When the Army turned him away for being under their height requirement of five feet eight inches, he simply found another path.

"The Air Force doesn't care how tall you are!" Ron would quote his brother with a grin, telling me how Laurie marched straight to their recruitment office. Those early Air Force days became family legends - everything borrowed from the Army at first, from their marching style to their paperwork.

Life threw them another curveball when a medical check-up revealed Laurie was colorblind.

"Most men would've given up right there," Ron would tell me proudly. "Not my brother. He just switched to cargo operations with the biscuit bombers. That was Laurie for you."

And then came Isabel - their unexpected wartime romance. "It was love at first sight," Ron would say, his eyes distant with the memory of his brother's story. When Laurie's ship had problems in the Channel and returned to port, they seized their chance and married right there in England.

But wartime romances came with their own particular heartaches. The military had strict rules about transport home - servicemen first, wives when possible. I remember Ron describing how hard it was for Laurie to leave his new bride behind in England, promising to send for her as soon as he could. "So many war brides faced the same thing," Ron would say quietly. "Love found and then separated by duty." Watching Ron tell these stories, I could see how deeply his brother's experiences had touched him.

When Ron would talk about the family's time at the Morialta Children's Home, his voice would get very soft. The Baptist Church had helped arrange their placement there during one of the family's darkest times. That building still stands today - Ron would point it out whenever we drove past. "Mum tried so hard to keep us all together," he'd say, "but sometimes life doesn't give you many choices."

Being one of the younger children turned out to be a blessing in disguise for Ron at Morialta. The staff gave him special duties, looking after his baby sister, Betty. While the older kids would head off to Northern Summit for school each day, Ron got to stay behind with the seniors, helping with the daily chores. "Betty needed her big brother," he'd tell me, and I could hear in his voice how that responsibility had helped him cope with their situation. Even in those difficult times, the bonds of family remained strong.

Ron rarely spoke about how hard it must have been for Ada to make that decision to send her children to Morialta, but I could see the understanding in his eyes whenever it came up. They all knew she'd done what she had to do to give them a chance at a better future. Sometimes, love means making the hardest choices of all.

Ron told me so many stories about his time at Morialta. Life there ran like clockwork - every morning, he'd be up early to milk the cows in the crisp dawn air, then help muster cattle across the grounds. When fruit season came, everyone pitched in with the picking. He and the other children had found this clever little shortcut to school, though Ron would chuckle when he admitted it didn't always keep them from being late. The weekends brought a different routine - his sister Wilma would take care of little Betty while Ron joined the older children with their regular chores.

"Thank heavens it didn't last longer than nine months," Ron would say whenever he talked about Morialta. None of the children were pleased there, even though they had everything they needed. His mother, Ada, felt the separation like a physical ache - Ron told me how she'd practically count the days until she could bring them home. "It wasn't that they were cruel to us," he'd explain, "but it just wasn't home." You could still hear the echo of those days in his voice when he talked about it, even years later.

The school was a mixed bag for young Ron. His eyes would light up when he talked about Geography and History lessons - how they transported him to distant lands and epic moments in time, far beyond their corner of South Australia. But then he'd groan, remembering his battles with Mathematics. "And spelling!" he'd laugh, shaking his head. "No matter how hard I studied, those words just wouldn't behave themselves."

The polio outbreak during his fourth-grade year added another worry to their already challenging lives. Ron remembered how it cast a shadow over their community, already struggling under the weight of the Depression. But he had such a wonderful spirit - even when telling me about those difficult times, he'd focus on how they made the best of things.

One of my favourite stories was about his childhood business ventures. He and the other children would gather sour sobs to sell for a penny a bunch - not much money, but every penny helped in those days. And then there were the yabbying expeditions to Brownhill Creek! Ron's eyes would sparkle as he described those adventures - two hours of walking to get there, just thirty precious minutes of actual yabbying, then an hour and a half trudging back downhill. "But oh, those yabbies made it all worthwhile," he'd say with a grin. Young Ron was already learning the value of hard work and making his own way in the world.

Listening to these stories, I could picture him as a boy - determined, resourceful, already showing the strength of character that would later draw me to him. Even in those challenging times, his natural optimism and enterprising spirit shone through.

Ron's first proper job was at a chicken farm near his home. He loved telling me about learning the precise art of egg collecting and cleaning. "You weren't allowed to touch them directly," he'd explain with a smile, "which seemed silly to me as a boy, but now I understand why." That job taught him more than just handling eggs—it was his first taste of real responsibility.

The Edwardstown Institute held such a special place in Ron's family life. His mother, Ada, bless her heart, never touched a drop of alcohol in her life, but she stayed active in the RSL after losing her husband. Ron would describe their regular family walks from Leonard Street up South Road to get to the Institute for club activities. He'd always chuckle when telling me about the time they moved to the refurbished building in the railway yard. "Poor Mum nearly fell over when she saw they'd put in a bar on the opening night!" he'd say. "Nobody had thought to warn her about that little addition."

It was at the Institute that Ron discovered his love for electric light cricket. Watching him describe those games, I could see how much they meant to him - not just the sport itself, but the feeling of being a normal boy for a while, free from the weight of being a war widow's son.

The story of Ron's time working at Gershwin's farm permanently moved me deeply. Gersh himself was quite a character - "like a force of nature," Ron would say, "though his wife was as gentle as he was fierce." She and Ada got along wonderfully. Ron would work from sunrise to sunset, proving himself so capable that he earned an extra five pounds weekly for outperforming the other workers during his first season.

But then came the harvest, and with it, a test of Ron's growing confidence. When Gersh tried to take away his bonus, claiming it should be shared with workers who were now starting earlier and finishing later, Ron found the courage to stand his ground. "I was terrified," he once admitted to me, "but I knew it wasn't right." His voice would fill with quiet pride when he told me how, by the next payday, Gersh had acknowledged his mistake.

That was my Ron - even as a young man, he had such a strong sense of fairness. It wasn't just about the money; it was about being treated with respect. Watching him tell these stories, I could see how these early experiences had shaped him into the man I would fall in love with.

After Gershwin's, Ron moved on to work at a stud farm with sheep - though he always smiled when telling me how he didn't have to look for the job himself. They'd actually headhunted him! I could tell he was rather proud of that, especially since he'd been so ready to leave Gersh's place behind. At the stud farm, he mainly worked with old man Geer and his sons - Mrs Geer rarely made an appearance. Ron would often say how much he learned about sheep farming during that time, his eyes lighting up when he talked about the different breeds and their characteristics.

Whenever Ron described farming in those days, I'd marvel at how different it was from modern operations. "Real horsepower," he'd say with emphasis, "not the kind you get from engines!" He painted such vivid pictures of those early morning routines - catching and harnessing the horses, a skill in itself. The poor animals needed frequent changes as they were tired from the heavy work. "You didn't just work on a farm back then," he'd tell me, "you lived and breathed it, every hour of every day."

One of my favourite stories was about Ron's encounter with what Bryce called a "21-pound crowbar." Ron's eyes would always twinkle when he told this one. Bryce had sent him running to fetch this supposedly essential tool, though Ron was suspicious - he knew crowbars usually topped out at 14 pounds. "When I finally found that 'crowbar,'" he'd laugh, "it turned out to be a massive post I could barely lift!" He suspected Bryce had played a little trick on him, probably managing to hold up one end of the tractor himself while Ron struggled with the post. Being smaller in stature, these physical challenges stuck in Ron's memory.

Ron stayed at Gerche's for nearly three full seasons - almost three years of his life. Though Gersh had been a demanding boss, Ron would often say he learned so much from him about the kind of farmer he wanted to become. And despite not being able to match Bryce's impressive strength, Ron took away valuable lessons from him, too. "I figured out pretty quick," he'd tell me, "that being a good farmer wasn't just about how much you could lift - it was about being clever, adaptable, and learning from every challenge that came your way."

Watching Ron share these memories, I could see how those farming years had shaped him, teaching him resilience and determination. Even when telling stories about the most challenging days, there was always a hint of pride in his voice

- pride in having overcome each challenge and learned from it.

Ron had a good relationship with the RSL and Legacy from his earliest days. His father had helped establish the Kalangadoo RSL as one of its original committee members, and after his passing, these organisations became lifelines for the family. When they moved to their Edwardstown house, which had suffered under previous tenants, both groups stepped in to help keep an eye on the family and make sure they stayed afloat.

Ron often told me about his mother Ada's dedication to the RSL, even though she never touched a drop of alcohol in her life. "She'd march us up South Road from Leonard Street," he'd say, describing their weekly trips to the Edwardstown Institute for club activities. I always smiled when he'd tell the story about Ada's shock at discovering they'd put a bar in their refurbished building in the railway yard. "Poor Mum had no idea they'd be serving alcohol there!" he'd chuckle. However, his voice would soften with admiration for how she stayed committed to the organisation despite her personal beliefs.

I remember Ron talking about the day Legacy stood up for him as he queued for secondhand textbooks. His eyes would always soften when he described standing in line, a small boy who had just lost his father. 'They called out that I was a Legacy child,' he'd say, 'and I was getting new books.' It wasn't just about the books, you know. It was about being seen, about someone recognising that he mattered during a time when he felt most alone.

He'd tell me how the loud announcement made him feel - not embarrassed, but almost proud. Like the world was saying, 'We've got your back, little one.' For a child who had lost everything, those new schoolbooks were more than just paper and ink. They were a promise that he wasn't forgotten, that there were people who cared. 'No one can really understand,' he'd say, 'what it means to a child to be given something new, something just for them, when everything else feels lost.'"

When Ron and I established our business together, I watched with such pride as he found ways to give back to the organisations that had supported his family through those difficult early years. Over those 10-11 years, he became Legacy's largest individual hands-on donor, contributing around half a million dollars. I remember how he'd work with those excellent Italian builders who'd built up their family company to include everything needed for house construction - from electricians to plumbers and everyone in between.

The way Ron leveraged his community connections to help Legacy touched my heart deeply. He never forgot how these organisations had helped his family when they needed it most, and being able to return that kindness meant everything to him. Watching him work so tirelessly to raise those funds, I could see that same determined spirit that had gotten him through those challenging childhood years, now channelled into helping others facing similar struggles.

For Ron, it wasn't just about the money—it was about honouring his father's memory and supporting the organisations that had been there for his family during their darkest times. Every donation and fundraising effort was his way of saying thank you and ensuring that other families would receive the same support he had gotten all those years ago.

Ron's dedication to Legacy led him to serve as president for "A Term," with Ken stepping in as his reliable deputy. During that time, Ron and Ada created something truly special - a widows' travel club. I loved how they included the Japanese war brides who had married service members after the war. These remarkable women, some of them Legacy widows themselves, became such a wonderful part of our community. It didn't matter one bit that they had once been considered "enemy" nationals - they were part of our Legacy family now.

I remember Ron telling me about Legacy's beginnings in Australia - how it started in Victoria in 1923 and reached South Australia by 1928. His family had come under Legacy's protective wing in 1931 when his father passed away. Ron always admired how Legacy insisted on being self-funded rather than relying on government support. "When help wasn't coming from outside," he'd say, "they just rolled up their sleeves and did it themselves."

The Legacy connection runs deep in our family. Ron and I were called Nana and Grandpa Clark—we were inseparable in their community service work. We travelled to Legacy events together for years, right up until I had an awful fall at an event in Henrick, New South Wales, when I was about 80. I remember how worried everyone was—Raelene and Lel flew straight to meet me, and thank goodness for Paul (Laurie's son), who helped arrange the air ambulance to bring me home.

The way Ron and these organisations have helped war widows and their children, regardless of where they came from, shows what real community support looks like. I couldn't be prouder of his dedication to continuing this vital mission. Every time I see him working with Legacy, I'm reminded of that young boy who once benefited from their help, now making sure other families get the same support he received all those years ago.

Ron never brags about being Legacy's largest individual hands-on donor—for him, it was never about recognition. What matters to him is knowing he helped other veterans' families, just as Legacy had once helped his own.

www.ingramcontent.com/pod-product-compliance
Lightning Source LLC
Chambersburg PA
CBHW032014050726
47590CB00006B/2169